Praise for Life Beyond 70.

Written in a loving, entertaining and highly informative style, *Life Beyond 70* covers a wide range of questions, concerns and solutions following the authors' lifetimes of in-depth experience. It is a "must read" for anyone living life beyond 70, as well as for those associating with or caring for anyone in this age group.
      --Iain (84)

Thank you for your incredible book! It shares many insightful suggestions on how to assist and care for our loved ones as they age. We can also reference it often to provide solid tips on growing old gracefully.
      --Heidi (78)

Life Beyond 70 is a delightful, useful, and easy to read book based not only on good, old fashioned common sense, but is backed up by personal experiences of the authors. A very worthwhile read for anyone dealing with the inevitable transition to old age.
      --Chuck (85) and Marlene (86)

I heartily endorse and recommend this practical, timely book to every family with aged loved ones who are looking for suggestions on how to make their lives productive and happy to the end.
      --John (86)

"Life beyond Seventy", is a very good source of helpful and practical information for those who are aging themselves, and those who become caregivers when their assistance is necessary. It is an interesting read with helpful ideas to increase one's confidence in knowing the help you are giving is likely adequate and fulfilling for the person. After being a caregiver for many years, now I am the one needing the help of my family and the facility where I live. I appreciate knowing my situation and needs are similar to others in the same circumstances.
  --Theo (93)

I highly recommend this book. I have worked in the geriatric arena with both Rich and Kim and know them to be wise and insightful in helping aged individuals make decisions. I wish I had had this book years ago to help my parents.
  --Judy (83)

Rich and Kim Condie offer a delightful look on the aging process. Anyone who is approaching 70 or beyond will find their book insightful and thought provoking. Each chapter successfully helps the reader to realize that aging can be a joyful journey. My husband and I read this book together and enjoyed discussing each chapter.   We would highly recommend this book to all.
  --John and Christelle (68 and 66)

Life Beyond 70

Life Beyond 70

Cheerful Direction
&
Gentle Nudges

For the Elderly
&
Those Who Care for Them

Richard Condie and Kim Condie

Chase Franklin Publishing

Copyright © 2023 Richard D. Condie and Leslie Kim Condie

All rights reserved. No part of this book may be reproduced in any form or by any means without permission in writing from the publisher. For information address Chase Franklin Publishing, P.O. Box 421, Bountiful, UT 84011.

First printing in paperbound edition, May 2024.

For information about special discounts for bulk purchases, please contact Chase Franklin Publishing at info@lifebeyond70.com

Cover design by Jason Condie

Library of Congress Cataloging-in-Publication Data
Condie, Richard D.
Condie, Leslie Kim
    Life Beyond 70
Library of Congress Control Number: 2023922145

ISBN   979-8-9893961-0-8 (paperback)
ISBN   979-8-9893961-1-5 (eBook)
ISBN   979-8-9893961-2-2 (audio book)

Printed in the United States of America

Dedicated to our parents:

Dolan and Shirley Condie
and
Paul and Della Mae Rasmussen

We love them. We appreciate them. We miss them.
We wish this book were available when we were
caregivers for them

CONTENTS

	Introduction	1
1	Adding Meaning To Your Life	7
2	Aging Gracefully	25
3	Counting Your Blessings	33
4	Exercising As We Age	39
5	Enjoying Elderly Grandparenthood	45
6	Adjusting To Dependency	55
7	Addressing Loneliness	79
8	Marriage At My Age?	91
9	Dispelling Worries	101
10	Calming Storms	121
11	Moving On	131
12	Managing Healthcare	135
13	Now, What Was His Name?	157
14	Writing Your Final Chapter	163
15	Smelling The Roses	175
	Quotes	179

Introduction

When Rich's parents, Dolan and Shirley, were in their 80s, we took them to lunch at a popular pizza restaurant. Suffering from Parkinson's, Shirley's balance was poor, and she needed a cane to provide stability. After placing their orders, Shirley indicated she needed to visit the ladies' room. Kim, wanting to ensure Shirley's safety, went with her. The women's restroom had only two stalls, and Kim waited by the sinks for her. Unfortunately, when Shirley was ready to come out, the latch on the stall was stuck. Although she worked on the fastener for several minutes, Shirley did not have the hand strength to get it open.

By now, two other women were waiting to use the stall. Realizing there was no other option, Kim concluded that she would have to open the door herself. The stall was relatively close to the floor, so Kim laid down on her stomach in front of the door. She then did the breaststroke on the restroom floor until she could scoot underneath.

Contorting to avoid both the toilet and Shirley, Kim stood and easily unlocked the latch. When the door swung open, the two waiting women stared with wide eyes and open mouths. They clearly had no response to what they had just witnessed. Shirley, acting as if this type of thing happened every day, moved over to the sinks to wash her hands. Kim, grateful to be off the bathroom floor, felt compelled to wash her hands as well. As they returned to the booth with the men, Kim wondered if her mother-in-law might be embarrassed by the experience. Instead, Shirley saw the humor in what had had happened. Upon returning to the table, Shirley announced, "Guess what just happened to me!" She then proceeded to share the story to the laughter of all four of us.

The aging process can regularly place both the elderly and the caregiver in unprecedented situations. Some can be funny. Most are more serious. And of course, many are life-altering or even life-threatening. No one can simply ignore what is happening. Pretending that we will never get old does not work.

Leaving the teenage years to become a functioning adult required a monumental change in our perspective. Thereafter, moving from our 20s to our 30s, 40s, and 50s required certain modifications. But the scale of the adjustments within our adult years was generally less onerous than when we moved from being a teenager. Life beyond seventy, however, no longer represents smooth sailing with small course corrections. The necessary changes when we become elderly are reminiscent in magnitude of our arrival into adulthood. We only get to be old once, so

Introduction

many of the challenges for the elderly are new, to both us and to caregivers who support us.

Although every person's circumstances are unique, many of the challenges are, in fact, common to aging. Each of the fifteen chapters in the book addresses a different set of issues facing those who are elderly. Often, seniors and their families are caught off guard as age-related problems begin to surface. These trials frequently come in waves with new tests arriving in short succession. While these difficulties are sometimes formidable, the elderly years can be amazing, satisfying, and filled with joy. In this book, we address many age-connected tribulations providing direction, encouragement, and hope.

This book, in fact, speaks to three different groups of readers. The first are those who are seniors by their age only. This group enjoys relatively good health and has no need for caregivers. Living independently, they anticipate the aging complexities that are yet to come. If the readers in this group are seventy, they have, on average, 15 years of remaining life because the life expectancy of a 70-year-old American today is about 85.

At some point, this first group will gradually slide into becoming the second, which includes those in the throes of the elderly trials. Health issues increase in intensity. Remaining independent becomes less of an option. Everyday life shifts to being more complicated. Help from caregivers is needed and appreciated.

The third type of readers is the caregiver themselves. Anyone of any age providing support to an elderly person qualifies for this group. Children, grandchildren, neighbors, and friends can all play the role. Spouses, even when suffering from their own aging tests, are often the primary caregivers to their partner. Caregivers take on increasing importance as the elderly advance. All three groups of readers are participating in the aging process.

> ## *Thoughts for Caregivers*
> When we shift to talking to caregivers, our suggestions will be highlighted in a "Thoughts for Caregivers" box. While most caregiver solutions do not involve doing the breaststroke on the floor of a public restroom, this book provides encouragement and perspective to those who assist the elderly.

The two of us behind this book are husband and wife. Now, we are the ones in our elderly years as both of us are in our seventies. When we were children, 70 was the average life expectancy for Americans. In those days, we did not think much about living into our seventies and beyond. But now we both have survived past that once-significant benchmark year.

For several decades, we have worked closely with hundreds of people who consider themselves elderly. Many lived independently. Others stayed with family or friends. Some resided in senior living centers. In three different regions of America, we assisted and encouraged individuals who were adjusting to the aging process. We know the challenging problems an elderly person is facing. We have witnessed solutions that successfully address these difficulties. Life beyond 70 is not always easy, but practical

Introduction

answers exist to achieve productive and meaningful lives. The remaining years of our lives can be some of our best.

Why 70? Why not 65 or 80? While any of those ages could have worked in writing this book, we find that beyond 70 years old, things usually begin to change. Initially, we might feel closer to our 60s than our 80s. Each of us ages differently. At some point, however, the aging process will become evident for each of us. Most feel dramatically older at 80 than when they were younger. All feel quite old at 90. But some become elderly at 55 or 60. The number, itself, does not matter. If we keep having birthdays, we will all eventually become "old." For us personally, we felt significantly older at 70 than we did at 65. So, we picked 70 as a starting point.

Please note that, although we are Christians, the book is non-denominational. So, while not espousing any doctrines about life and death, our perspectives are based on Christian beliefs.

Also, we are Americans who have spent most of our lives in the United States. We fully recognize that some details of our suggestions relate to opportunities and resources specific to the USA. We believe, however, that the overall challenges of aging are universal and common to people in most cultures. We hope our friends in other lands, both those that are aging as well as those who are caregiving, will find perspective and hope through this book.

All the best,

Rich and Kim Condie

Thoughts to ponder:

What would I like to get out of this book?

_____

_____

_____

_____

_____

_____

_____

_____

Chapter 1

Adding Meaning To Your Life

Kim's father's was confined to a hospital bed for the last four years of his life. During those years, Rich and his father-in-law spoke frequently on the phone and enjoyed a great relationship. At one point, Paul asked Rich how the operation of his candy factory was performing.

"Not very well." Rich responded.

Paul, a Caltech-educated engineer, replied that he would love to come and help. Recognizing that Paul could not be of much assistance from his hospital bed and understanding that Paul could never make either a flight or a 12-hour drive to get to our home, Rich thought the offer was just wishful thinking. He expressed gratitude for the proposed aid and expected the issue to simply go away.

Thirty minutes later, Rich received an alarmed call from Kim's mom. Della Mae told Rich that he needed to immediately speak with Paul. Her husband was convinced that the two of them needed to drive the 800 miles to our home so that he could help Rich with his factory. She tried explaining to Paul that he could neither fly nor help with the driving duties. And she could not possibly drive for the 12 hours needed to get there. Anticipating her response, Paul had a ready solution. He told her that she only needed to drive for one hour each day. They would then stop and check into a motel until the next morning. If they repeated that effort for 12 days, they would eventually get there. He was insistent that, "Rich needs me. So, we must go." Rich asked her to hand the phone to Paul.

"Paul, you can't come to help."

"Why not?"

"Because Della Mae is not up to it."

Dejectedly, he conceded that she was probably not strong enough to make the drive. Rich thanked him for his willingness to help.

As we age, each of us wants to remain relevant. We want to contribute. We desire to be needed. We want to maintain meaning in our lives. Paul's heartfelt offer, delivered from his hospital bed of several years, reflects the fervor of someone who truly desired to be of service.

Midlife is a busy time of making a living, raising kids, seeking entertainment, etc. Once we become older, the heavy demands of our middle years subside. With more time on our hands, we contemplate what life has left to offer and what difference we can still make. Let's consider how we can add purpose and value to the last chapters of our life.

When I grow up…

When we were young, we often projected ahead and speculated about what we wanted to become when we "grew up." Our musings were focused on careers, accomplishments, education, or relationships. We changed our direction several times as we matured. However, now that we have moved beyond middle age, our early-year goals are behind us. So, how do we adjust our thinking about what lies ahead? Do we have any ambitions for our remaining years? Do we have a bucket list? Can we still "become" something new or something better?

Let us throw out some suggestions for consideration:

- Become an artist. Take up watercolors. Paint landscapes. Sketch portraits.
- Become an author. Write a children's book or a novel. Pen a short story. Create a cookbook.
- Become a linguist. Learn a new language.
- Become a poet. Regularly generate new poems.
- Become a difference maker. Find new ways to serve others.
- Become a musician. Learn a new instrument or pick up an old instrument you used to play.
- Become a builder or craftsperson. Make something with your hands.
- Become a teacher. Help a struggling young student. Teach English to immigrants. Share your talents with those interested in learning.

- Become a walker, hiker, or jogger. Run or walk in a 5k race, or longer.

The options of what we can become are different than our career or vocation and can be limitless. Use your senior years to become something new.

Kim's mother was a college professor at a large university with a PhD in psychology. Della Mae was well respected in her field. She authored books in her area of expertise as well as many children's books. Yet, in her seventies, she reinvented herself in a totally unexpected way. She and a female neighbor friend put together a delightful vaudeville act. Wearing clown costumes with colored wigs and red noses, the two women danced and sang while sharing jokes that Della Mae had collected throughout her life. They performed their act several times, generally to amused women's groups. Unfortunately for us, we lived out of state when these performances took place. Oh, how we wish we could have witnessed their act. But in their honor, let us add one more possibility to the above list of things you might consider, "Become a vaudeville performer."

Before leaving the thought of what you might become, let us add one more outside-the-box idea. The 1,000-mile Alaskan Iditarod dog-sled race is one of the most grueling events imaginable. The race is held every March in the wilderness of central Alaska and continues no matter how bad the weather conditions. Wind-chills of 80 below, blinding blizzards, waist-deep snow, and terribly rough terrain are deemed to be normal. Angry attacking moose are not uncommon. Taking care of a dozen high-strung dogs is part of the daily routine. A sustained adrenaline rush offsets

Adding Meaning To Your Life

sleep deprivation. This event is clearly best suited for younger people. Yet one 83-year-old man completed the race after previously failing twice. Despite suffering broken ribs, falling through the ice into a river, and a broken sled, he completed the race in 21 days and 10 hours. While becoming an Iditarod dog race participant is not likely to be of interest to most of our readers, the fact that this man actually completed the race is an inspiration for us to think differently about what is possible.

If the craziness of the Iditarod pushes the thought of what you might become far beyond your comfort level, let us suggest a different approach. Instead of "becoming something new," you might want to consider "becoming something better" by refining and improving personal character traits.

You could:

- Become more patient.
- Become more flexible.
- Become kinder.
- Become more considerate.
- Become a better listener.
- Become more determined.
- Become calmer.
- Become less angry.
- Become more forgiving.
- Become more grateful.
- Become a better spouse or friend or caregiver.
- Become a better parent, grandparent, great-grandparent, or sibling.

Every person has areas of opportunity in their character that could use some work. One way to use our senior years productively is to choose to become a better person.

We had a dear friend who we first met in his late 80s. If ever he was asked to do something, his response was always the same, "Consider it done!" And so it was. If you choose to become something better at your age, begin with the adage, "Consider it done!"

The opposite of "becoming something" might be sliding into inactivity or allowing our troubles to dictate the future of our remaining life chapters. The elderly years can be trying with health challenges and less energy than when we were younger.

To keep moving forward, you may want to avoid:
- Focusing on how lonely you are.
- Complaining about everything.
- Watching the news constantly.
- Sleeping the days away.
- Not trying.
- Letting others do everything for you.
- Binge-watching TV all day.

Especially in the senior years when the time requirements of middle age have subsided, the opportunity to become something new or something better is particularly good. Use your precious time remaining to achieve worthwhile goals. The effort will shift your focus away from your age-related challenges.

We fully recognize that a time will come when our options to become something new or something better will become more limited. One wise observer of the elderly said,

"When you cannot do what you've always done, you do what matters most." We agree.

Happiness

Many would conclude that the purpose of life is to be happy. During Rich's career, he spent many years working with several billionaires. Some of the wealthiest people were the most miserable people he ever met. Their extreme wealth did not make them the slightest bit happy. They desired that everyone that worked for them become as despondent as they were. Similarly, a person's age does not in any way correspond with their level of personal happiness. Some of the happiest people we know are some of the oldest.

So, wealth and age seem to have no correlation with one's level of happiness. A person's contentment is more a reflection of their attitude than the circumstances surrounding them.

An American volunteer in Africa observed that the locals "by the world's measure.... have little --- except happiness. By contrast, many of us have everything --- except happiness." One wise older man summarized the situation perfectly when he said, "I find it is better to count my blessings than to recount my problems." An astute senior woman remarked, "The only way to get through life is to laugh your way through it. You either have to laugh or cry. I prefer to laugh. Crying gives me a headache."

The thesaurus lists synonyms for happiness as pleasure, gladness, cheerfulness, joy, glee, bliss, delight, exhilaration, and ecstasy. To add complexity to this definition, we can experience both happiness and sadness at the same time. Life has ups and downs. When times are good, we can still experience disappointments. Conversely, we can remain joyful, even when stretches of life are difficult. When the challenges of age are pounding us, it helps to remind ourselves to seek to be happy.

Make a Difference

Few of us in life get our likeness carved into a Mount Rushmore. But lives well lived, even in our last chapters, can continue to favorably impact others. When Rich's mother died, we were moved by how many of the workers in her senior living center seemed genuinely sad at her passing. Even in her last years, Shirley succeeded in making a difference.

When Kim was young, her great-grandmother, in her nineties, came to live with Kim's grandparents. Her eyesight was gone. She wanted, however, to contribute as best she could. So, she volunteered to do the dishes. In the days before dishwashers, every dish and utensil from every meal was washed, rinsed, and dried by hand. She could not see the food on the dishes, but she could feel it. So, by touch, she carefully cleaned each article. Kim remembers her cheerfully standing at the kitchen sink carrying out her responsibilities. She made a difference in others' lives.

Rich's grandmother was a teacher in a small rural school, whose former early-grade students frequently came back to see her in later years. Almost every time Rich visited his grandparents' home, at least one of these former students would unexpectedly knock on their door. Each was warmly embraced and invited into her home to reminisce about their time together. Did they remember her? Absolutely. Kim's grandfather was also a teacher, but at the high-school level. No matter where he went in his later life, people stopped him in public places to express their appreciation for his contribution to their growing-up years. He always took the time needed to reconnect to those who remembered him.

All of us have people in our lives that we warmly remember. Some were elderly at the time we interacted with them. What can we do to enrich the lives of those with whom we interact? How can we make a meaningful difference to those who are younger than we are?

Recording Your Life History

Most of us will not have biographers chronicle the history of our lives. If we do not record our own life narrative, our past will be unknown to our posterity. Stories of our lives help future generations to understand the circumstances in which we lived and give them inspiration for their own lives. Either we must record our own life history, or it will vanish as we leave this world.

We lived in far-away states from Rich's parents during most of our married lives. He talked with them regularly, and we visited them once a year. When we eventually moved to the state where they lived, we did more things with them. But one thing stands out to us now. Every Memorial Day, we drove them several hours to the small farming community where they grew up. We left flowers in three different cemeteries. We got fresh strawberry milkshakes from the drive-through burger place. But most importantly, they told stories of their growing-up years. Consequently, we learned many details of their youth that we had not previously understood. Now that they are gone, what a blessing those annual trips were.

Separately, both of Rich's parents prepared small paperback books full of photos and stories about their lives. Each bound paperback was approximately 4" by 6" and had about 50 pages. Dolan had two books, and Shirley had one. The histories are easy to read for even younger grandchildren (and great grandchildren). In contrast, lengthy comprehensive life histories written by well-meaning seniors are generally too tedious for one's posterity to find interesting. Stories are appealing; exhaustive details can be boring.

Rich's grandmother spoke into a tape recorder to document anecdotes from her life. Even today it is fun to hear her voice. Rich was asked to speak at her funeral and chose to play a story she had recorded. Consequently, she "spoke" at her own funeral. Nothing he could have said would have been as delightful and well received as the story she told in her own voice. Today there are many ways you can record stories, including on mobile phones and online applications.

Rich's mom grew up on a farm on the outskirts of a small town during the Great Depression. They had plenty to eat, but Shirley's father had to drive over 100 miles on dirt roads to access employment. When Christmas came around, money for presents or even a tree did not exist. In her stocking, which was hung over the fireplace, young Shirley found an orange. No toys. No candy. Just a single orange. When she told the story, Shirley was not complaining. No bitterness or frustration was in her voice. Times were tough. She was quite happy to have an orange. Your posterity would most likely delight in knowing how you celebrated holidays.

Shirley also shared a story of going to a high school event in her small town several miles from the farm where she grew up. After the event, she and a girlfriend walked together in the dark along the dirt road toward their homes. About halfway home, the friend peeled off onto a side road leaving Shirley to walk alone for the remainder of the journey. At some point, car lights could be seen headed from town in her direction. Even though she probably knew every person who might be traveling that road, Shirley became afraid. She jumped into the irrigation ditch along the side of the road until the car passed. Visualizing Rich's mom as a high school girl hiding in a dark ditch is a delightful memory of her. Telling younger people about your youthful fears would be fascinating to them.

One aged widower wrote a three-page document of the hardships of daily life in mining camps where he grew up. He included a story about moving to an older house with no access to running water. The house had an empty "cistern" dug vertically in the yard. The water tank was ten feet deep and four feet in diameter with a cement floor. He could not remember if it had dirt walls. To "clean" it, he was lowered into the cistern by his father where he removed a dead gopher and two dead rats. He tidied it up a bit before being pulled back out. The family then brought buckets of water from a nearby irrigation ditch to slowly fill up the tank. After letting the dirt settle for a couple of days, the cistern became their source for drinking water. This man's children and grandchildren were delighted to learn more about the primitive challenges in his early years.

Many experiences in your youth would be of interest to your offspring.

Here are some areas they might find fascinating:
- Life during the Great Depression. Everyday struggles during WWII. The Korean and Vietnam Wars and their impact on everyday life. Your feelings and experiences regarding 9/11.
- Party-line telephones and long-distance calls. The roles of radios and phonographs. Life without microwave ovens, clothes dryers, or televisions. Coal-stoves in the kitchen, woodstoves for heating a room, and huge coal-burning furnaces.
- Polio. Dentist visits before Novocain. Smallpox vaccinations.
- Necco Wafers and Mary Janes. Popcorn popped in a pot on the stove.
- Walking five miles to and from school in the snow uphill both ways. Milk deliveries to your home.
- Out-houses and chamber pots. Baths in a metal tub in the kitchen. Making a hot-water bottle to bed to warm your feet.
- The Sears and Roebuck Catalog – especially the Winter/Christmas Edition.

Just because you have fond memories of your childhood heroes, do not assume your posterity knows who they are.

Adding Meaning To Your Life

Share with your family who impacted your thinking in your younger years.

Perhaps some of these famous people might have been important to you:
- Shirley Temple, Fred Astaire, Sammy Davis Jr., Benny Goodman, Lawrence Welk, Ella Fitzgerald, Nat King Cole, Ed Sullivan, Johnny Carson, The Beatles
- Babe Ruth, Joe DiMaggio, Jackie Robinson, Jessie Owens, Joe Namath, Jim Brown, Bill Russell, John Wooden
- Eleanor Roosevelt, Marion Anderson, Dwight Eisenhower, Helen Keller, John F. Kennedy, Mr. Rogers

Your children and grandchildren know very little about your personal history. If you do not share your own stories, these tales will be lost forever. Find a way to get them recorded or written. Get help from family members, if needed, or hire someone to transcribe your words. Talk about your own parents and grandparents as well. Old photographs need to be labeled. Write the names of each person on the back of the photos, the year if you have it, and even a memory. All this history will be lost if you do not record it.

Know Your Roots

We are a composite of our ancestors. We are who we are, living where we do, because of decisions and sacrifices they made decades and even centuries before. A Hawaiian woman recently became interested in learning more about her great grandmother who had contracted leprosy at the age of 24. Lepers in those days were all dropped off at the leper colony on the island Molokai. One can only imagine the horror of leaving your family and friends to enter a settlement with the other lepers. Fortunately, a young man of similar age had also contracted the horrid disease and had been moved to the colony 6 months before her. They courted and married. Within a year they had a child, a daughter. By law, children born in the leper colony had to be removed from the island before they turned one year old to avoid contracting the disease. Giving up their healthy child to be raised by someone else must have been devastating to the young couple. Sadly, they watched as the boat left with their toddler whom they would never see again. The couple had two more children, both of which died before they turned one. The first daughter became the grandmother to the woman doing the research. How grateful this woman was that she was able to learn about the sacrifices endured by her great grandparents. She very much enjoyed visiting her great grandmother's gravesite on Molokai.

One of the great movements of recent decades has been to learn more about our ancestors. Many resources, including DNA tests, are now available to research and find out more about our forbearers. Of the many available family history websites, we personally like the "Family Search" site, which is sponsored by the Church of Jesus Christ of Latter-day Saints. Anybody can set up a free account and access enormous amounts of information about their family tree. Through this site, you can also access other commercial family-history sites for free.

Adding Meaning To Your Life

(See the list of family-history websites at the end of this section.)

If you search for a relative, it is amazing how many types of records can be instantly accessed including census, birth, death, marriage, military, and immigration documents. If so inclined, you can add information, photos, or stories that you know about your own relatives. In his later years, Rich's dad set a goal of locating one new ancestor to add to his family tree every day. Dolan chose to delay watching TV each evening until he had accomplished his objective.

Family history is an area of interest for many elderly. You may find the connections to deceased relatives to be highly interesting. A small level of computer ability is required. But help with technology is available from family (including grandchildren), as well as community libraries.

Here are some family history websites you might find helpful:

- FamilySearch.org
- Ancestry.com
- Findmypast.com
- MyHeritageGeneanet.com
- Filae.com
- Google

Thoughts to ponder:

What would I like to become? Or how would I like to become better?

_____

_____

_____

_____

_____

_____

_____

_____

_____

How can I become happier? How can I make a difference?

_____

_____

Adding Meaning To Your Life

What are some of my life's stories that I want to record?

How can I learn more about my ancestors?

Chapter 2

Aging Gracefully

When Rich's mother was in her late 80s, she repeatedly fell and injured herself. Shirley's first fall broke her wrist, requiring surgery. After the first tumble, the common-sense solution to preventing further injuries from falls would have been to start using a walker. Nope. She refused. Without a walker to steady her balance, Shirley fell three more times over the next few years. Each time, she broke another bone. During that period, her decision to avoid a walker was consistent. Her unwavering explanation was, "A walker would make me look old." Given her age, that explanation seemed humorous to us. But it made perfect sense to her. She desired to look as young as possible, and a walker would conflict with her youthful appearance.

The concern voiced by Rich's mom is hardly unique. Many elderly make decisions based on that same rationale.

Who wants to look old? The choice to delay using a walker, for example, is a recurring pattern. While most do not wait until after their fourth fall with injuries, many choose to delay using a walker long after it would have been prudent to start. While the elderly may be aging, most do not want to appear old.

When Rich turned 50, his mother told him that she had no problem with her own age, but she struggled with the idea that she had a son who was fifty. Her comment, while thought provoking, was not entirely accurate. Shirley did have a problem with her own age. She had a problem with both of their ages. Over time, her frustration with her age subsided as it does for most elderly. She eventually came to recognize, as well as accept, that she too was aging. Shirley clearly enjoyed her later years, living comfortably into her nineties. Well, she is now gone, and we have children approaching the fifty-year milestone.

When we were children, our parents occasionally reminded us to, "Act your age." Their encouragement was intended to provide us with a burst of increased maturity. Sometimes it worked. Other times, we persisted in being children. The challenge to "act your age" returns to all of us as we grow older.

I Feel Younger Than My Age

Most elderly do not recognize their years accurately. We generally feel younger than our age, and we become seniors before we are ready. We are often surprised when the person looking back at us in the mirror appears far older than we expected. This mirror experience is not a one-time event. Mirror-shock can go on for years. The same disbelief happens when a candid photo is taken of us. Is that person really me? Do I always look that old? A corresponding surprise occurs when looking around a crowded room, and we realize that we are the oldest people present. We all grow old without recognizing it is happening.

As people age, they continue to think they can do things they could do when they were younger. Our family laughingly remembers a time when Rich's father, then about 70, tried to climb into a canoe from a dock on a lake. Our children were waiting to get in once Grandpa Dolan had stabilized the canoe. Unfortunately, instead of stepping into the middle, he put his weight on the side of the canoe. To everyone's surprise, Dolan was immediately dumped into the lake. He dropped down into the water leaving only his hat and the empty canoe floating on the surface.

Dolan could swim well, but he took a while to return to the surface. Embarrassed to have fallen into the water, he could not figure out how to gracefully ignore that his mishap had occurred. With only his hat visible in the water, the family waited anxiously for his head to bob to the top. The high school girl working the canoe rentals was becoming increasingly concerned. He finally swam up and climbed onto the dock.

Soaking wet, Dolan attempted to act as if nothing unusual had happened. Mercifully, his second attempt to enter the canoe was successful. The youngest grandchild, having observed what happened to Grandpa, then refused to get into the canoe.

Rich recently experienced a similar embarrassment. When given the choice to either float down the Animas River in Durango, Colorado in a raft with the younger grandkids, his daughter, and Kim, he opted to take an open kayak with the older grandsons and his son-in-law. This section of the river was quite tame except for a small 25-yard section with Class 3 rapids. Rich, 30 years earlier, had had no trouble maneuvering a kayak through those same rapids.

Just before the difficult stretch, the guide instructed the kayak riders how to enter and negotiate the rapids. The grandsons went first with no trouble navigating the run. Rich, however, quickly lost control, got turned around backwards, and was dumped out of the kayak. The life preserver kept him afloat as the river quickly pulled him through the brief rapids. Once through, however, with the kayak paddle in one hand and one of his sandals in the other, he made little progress in swimming the few yards to his kayak. Soon, the guide brought the kayak to him.

The other family members were amused by Rich's unsuccessful run through the rapids. Adding to their enjoyment were photos taken by the river-trip company of each person as they made their way through the rapids. In a series of photos, each step of Rich's misfortune was recorded in detail. All the family roared as they observed the photographic review of grandpa's misadventure.

Embarrassing moments like the canoe and kayak incidents are part of aging. Both Rich and his dad could laugh about these mishaps afterwards. These events are part of family tales told whenever family members gather. Age often catches us by surprise.

Aging Gracefully

One 85-year-old man had been a three-sport letterman in his youth at the University of Arizona. When provided an opportunity to join a backyard volleyball game with much younger adults, he assumed that he could still hold his own in such a game. He and everyone else quickly realized that he could no longer accurately time the hit of an oncoming volleyball. In fact, he could no longer even jump. The shock of his physical demise was devastating to him. Fortunately, he quickly retired to the sideline before injuring himself. Often, the last to recognize that a person has aged is, in fact, the person themselves.

Attending funerals can be a wakeup call as we age. Memorial services for parents are particularly hard. At these heart-felt events, we realize that we have become the oldest generation in our family. How did that happen? We do not feel as old as our parents appeared to be when they inherited the "oldest" family member title. For most, the aging process simply sneaks up on us. Since the clock never stops ticking, time marches on whether we accept it or not.

Aging Surprises

Since the aging process is new to each of us, we can be surprised by many of the unexpected changes. For instance, our memories of specific details of past experiences can gradually deteriorate. Our recollection of locations, events, and people can become, with time, a bit distorted. Even though we think we remember things vividly, those memories can be somewhat clouded from what actually happened. These fuzzy views can be particularly true for geographic sites.

Life Beyond 70

We had an experience with our grandchildren, which they found to be amusing. Like other teenagers getting close to graduating from high school, our grandchildren began considering what colleges they might want to attend. Consequently, we were asked to give our daughter's family a tour of the university campus that the two of us attended. Their family had previously visited a different college from which our daughter and her husband graduated. On that campus, they enjoyed a delightful student-led tour. Instead of signing up for such a guided tour of our college, they asked us to show them around the campus.

Unfortunately, we had not walked the university grounds in 40 years. Adding to our rusty memories were the many new buildings that had been erected, some of which replaced old buildings. As we wandered in a disorganized manner, we found ourselves disagreeing on the basic layout of the campus. The grandkids, as well as our daughter and her husband, became increasingly entertained by our muddled recollections and general confusion about the current campus. The contrast between our flawed university visit compared to the "professionally" guided tour of the other college site was on stark display. Subsequently, our grandchildren laughingly remind us of our pathetic attempt to sell them on our alma mater.

Another inevitable outcome of growing old is that we become shorter. We could easily see it in our parents as the years progressed. Recently, at our annual wellness exams, we too discovered the respective decline in our statures. Kim has lost 1 ¼" and Rich ¾" from when we were young. A whopping 2" between us has disappeared.... so far.

Aging Gracefully

So, what happens in the next decade, or the decade thereafter? We recently spoke to a dear friend who is now in her nineties. Always relatively short, she informed us with a smile that she now qualifies as "tiny." Overhearing that comment, her daughter responded, "Come on, 'Happy', we need to be going." Well, the elderly years throw each of us aging curveballs.

An additional consequence of the aging process is that we can become somewhat eccentric. For some reason, Rich has begun to grow rogue hairs on his face that defy his shaving skills. Also, he regularly finds his pant leg magically tucked into his sock. Even his fly occasionally remains unzipped. Kim and Rich have begun debating whether these lapses are "quirky" or "endearing" with Rich voting for the latter definition. So far, we have yet to reach an agreement on these classifications. But none-the-less, simple things that were once easy, seem with time, increasingly harder to navigate.

Acting Our Age

As we age, we all recoil against the thought of growing old. All are eventually forced to adjust their lifestyle to the frailties of the aging process. No one gets to go back in time. Once we begin to recognize and accept our age, we hope to become endearingly old as others observe our growing weaknesses. We are hardly the first to experience old age. We will certainly not be the last. Acting our age, whether as young children or as seniors, is a learned behavior that requires effort.

Thoughts to ponder:

What can I do to age gracefully?

Chapter 3

Counting Your Blessings

For most, a block of years is experienced beyond 70 before the toll of aging becomes severe. Often retired, generally empty-nesters, and hopefully in relatively good health, these years can be some of the best times of our lives. As we cross the 70-year threshold, our list of blessings is generally abundant. But as the years slide by, our good fortune can begin to somewhat fade.

A retired heart surgeon in his early eighties was watching a movie at home with his wife comfortably seated next to him. Suddenly and with no warning, she had a massive heart attack and immediately died. All his years of training and experience could not reverse the effects of that surprise assault on her heart. Despite a lifetime of helping others with heart disease, he was helpless to anticipate, let alone correct, his wife's problem. This sudden and unexpected change of circumstances highlights why each of us needs to appreciate our blessings as long as we still have them.

On a recent drive, we were enjoying the spectacular autumn leaves in a canyon when two high-speed police cars going the opposite direction zoomed by us with screaming sirens. Distracted by the two police vehicles flying by, Rich failed to see that the previously fast-moving traffic in front of us had come to a complete stop. Kim screamed, "Look out!" just in time for Rich to slam on the brakes and swerve to the right. Fortunately, no vehicles were in the traffic lane next to us. We screeched to a stop well before the cars now in front of us but beyond the vehicles in our original lane. If Rich had reacted a moment later, a catastrophic accident would have significantly altered our futures. One second, life was beautiful. Another second, our world would have turned upside down. How quickly our lives can dramatically change.

A few years back, a 75-year-old divorced friend called Rich to inform him that he had been diagnosed with a detached retina. While expressing appropriate concern, Rich inquired about the status of his other eye. Surprisingly, the man explained that he had no second eye. The friend's glass eye was so lifelike that Rich had never noticed that he could only see out of one eye. How did he lose the first one? A detached retina was the answer. As you can imagine, the man was duly concerned about losing the sight in his remaining eye. The fact that he lived alone added to his anxiety. Fortunately, a surgery successfully repaired his retina for which he was greatly relieved and profoundly grateful. His recovery process, however, included wearing a patch for several days thereby making him temporarily completely blind. When the healing process was finished, the friend had a new-found appreciation for the vision in his remaining eye.

One of the many potential outcomes of getting COVID was the temporary loss of the senses of smell and taste. For most, these senses eventually returned. But while gone, oh, how we missed those simple pleasures! Kim has a cousin who permanently lost his senses of smell and taste in his forties. While playing a game of pickup basketball, he sustained a concussion when his head hit the floor. His brain, thereby, disconnected his taste buds and smelling ability. Now, two decades later, those precious senses have never returned. Underappreciated by all who enjoy them, smelling and tasting are highly regarded if they evaporate.

Frequently, we do not value many of our most cherished blessings until they are withdrawn. A loving spouse, good health, family members including parents and siblings, enjoyable careers, dear friends, functioning eyesight and hearing, the ability to walk comfortably and safely, and driving privileges are some of the treasured assets that may eventually disappear. Part of growing old is the forfeiture of some blessings that we often do not esteem enough while they are available.

Losing some things dear to us can easily happen in our younger years. Long before we reach 70, trials of significant consequence can befall us. But beyond 70, the propensity for these types of occurrences increases. The years after we reach 80, or surely beyond 90, are filled with challenges that are often greater than what most of us experience in all our decades before 70. Gratitude for all that we have is needed for as long as these things are still ours. Let us take no blessing for granted.

Appreciating our current remaining blessings can help us deal with the aging trials. When Rich's mother was in her 90s, she became despondent after her husband was gone. Parkinson's, heart disease, and a host of other ailments frustrated her daily existence. Mourning her husband's passing added to her misery. She was encouraged to write down a list of her current blessings. She followed the suggestion and made a long list of things for which she was thankful. She kept the list on a lamp table next to her easy chair. Whenever she was down a little, she reread the gratitude list, which helped to improve her resolve to look for the positive and uplifting things in her life. Counting the blessings we still possess can help us deal with those that may have disappeared.

Thoughts to ponder:

What blessings are most important to me?

_____

_____

_____

_____

_____

Counting Your Blessings

Chapter 4

Exercising As We Age

At the funeral of a widow in his congregation, the minister shared a story that happened when the woman was in her seventies. At that point, she was already bent over with age. He related how he had strained his own back and could barely move during his regular Sunday services. Observing his discomfort, she marched up at the end of the meeting and asked to immediately see him in his office. He unsuspectingly followed her out of the chapel. Once the office door was closed, she told him to stand with his back to her. Before he knew what was happening, she had backed up to him, locked arms with him, and then pulled him forward onto her back. Fearing he might hurt her, he chose not to fight his way out of her arm holds. Even though he significantly outweighed her, she proceeded to bounce him up and down on her back. Finally, she released him placing his feet back on the ground.

Embarrassed by the experience, he was just glad that no one had observed her therapy on him. Did the treatment work? He remained so flustered by the event that he could not remember how his back responded. We, of course, would not suggest her assistance to the minister as a normal exercise routine. But she was clearly stronger than her bent over posture would suggest.

At some point before we turn seventy, most of us have cut back on what we did as teenagers. Contact sports such as tackle football, basketball, and wrestling are long gone. Mike Tyson recently signed up for a boxing match at 58, but he probably will not be climbing into the ring at 70. Golf, tennis, pickle ball, running, bowling, and swimming may be options for a while. Skiing, biking, and hiking can still work for a period. While you still can, exercise tailored to your individual circumstances and interests can contribute to your physical and mental wellness.

We have dear friends who exercise six days a week. The husband is 86 and the wife is 83. One day they ride their bikes. The next day, they do laps in the local community center swimming pool. A hike in the mountains comes after that. Then they start the rotation again. They feel good. They plan to continue this pattern as long as they can. We are younger, but once we sold our business, we started doing a similar exercise pattern, only without the lap swimming. But we also like to snowshoe when the snow is deep enough. We know other seniors who have their own personalized versions of exercise routines.

Jack LaLanne's widow, Elaine, was still working out every day at 96. Eventually, all of us, including presumably Elaine,

Exercising As We Age

will have to tone down the types of exercise we pursue. Here are some less onerous workout options to consider:

- Walking, even with a walker, is a simple form of exercise. When walking alone, you might try having a "goal" each day. One day look for colors. The next day listen for various sounds. Then seek for different smells. Make your walking activity into a game. We like to count the different wildflowers we see on hikes in the mountains. One widower met his second wife in a walking club. He proudly displayed his 1000-mile walking medallion.
- Stationary bikes become a safe method to exercise. There are even "peddlers" that a person can use while seated in their chair. Many in their nineties can still ride these types of bikes. But if you are still capable of riding a real bike, the fresh air would be an additional benefit.
- Classes for the elderly are often available at no cost at the local community recreation centers or online. Flexibility training can add much to the lives of the aging. Take an easy "Tai Chi" class for balance, flexibility, and mental relaxation. Exercising with someone else encourages consistency as well as sociability. If more aggressive programs no longer make sense, chair aerobics or chair yoga programs are available.
- Weight rooms at local recreation centers or senior living centers can help with needed strength exercises. Lifting weights at home can work as well. Kim's dad worked with one-pound weights in his

hospital bed for years. One elderly woman lifted water jugs at home. Her grandson, observing her jug-exercises, suggested that she should enter the "Senior Olympics" in her region. She took his advice and won an event in her age group.

- Join a seniors' dance group. Both sets of our parents belonged to dance clubs. One senior found his second, as well as his third wife, after joining dance groups.
- One foursome of men in their eighties enjoyed a weekly game of golf. Only one of the four, a former WWII Navy pilot, could see where the balls went. So, he had to watch where all four balls were hit. Fortunately, none of the foursome could drive the balls very far.
- Use the stairs if you can. On most days, one 94-year-old takes the stairs instead of the elevator at her senior living center.
- Gardening can even be exercise for the elderly. Plant some tomatoes, other vegetables, or herbs in either your backyard or in a flowerpot.

In a recent 100 Mile Race of the USA Track and Field Championship held in Nevada, amazingly, four of the 44 finishers were over 80 years old. The fastest of the four completed the run in just less than 30 hours setting a course record in his age group. So, how old is too old to compete in an ultra-distance race? We are not sure. But the answer is a lot older than we would have guessed.

The benefits of exercising are noteworthy. Be careful about appropriate age and health-related limitations.

Consult the experts if you are uncertain about starting up an exercise routine. But be consistent. As the saying goes, "Those that stop moving, stop moving. Those that keep moving, keep moving."

Thoughts to ponder:

What exercise efforts do I want to pursue?

_____

_____

_____

_____

_____

_____

Chapter 5

Enjoying Elderly Grandparenthood

Kim, at 65, was taking care of some of our grandchildren while our daughter and her husband traveled. At one point, Kim was sitting on the sidelines of one grandchild's soccer game next to the youngest grandson, Bentley, a delightful 5-year-old. To entertain the boy, who was clearly bored watching his sibling play, Kim suggested they play a guessing game. They took turns giving hints to each other until the object or person in mind could be identified.

At one point, Kim said, "I am thinking of a person. He has a deep belly laugh, sparkling eyes, and red hair."

Bentley responded, "I know who it is! It's me!"

"You're right!", she agreed.

He then continued, "I am thinking of a person who is very, very, VERY old." He emphasized the third "very".

Kim responded, "I know who it is! It's me!"

"You're right!", Bentley excitedly replied.

If Bentley believed that "Gram" was very, very, VERY old at 65, wait until she added even more years to her total.

We have 16 grandchildren ranging from college age to newborn. We found that grandparenting in our fifties and sixties can be very enjoyable. Being an elderly grandparent, however, often requires a few modifications. Generally, your grandchildren are getting older and could even be parents themselves before you are gone. Some of your grandchildren and great-grandchildren may have trouble relating to a person as old as you are. And the chaos of small children can become less comfortable for us as we age. Being an elderly grandparent can be a bit daunting.

We certainly do not have all the answers, but let us share some thoughts:

- Love your grandchildren and great-grandchildren unconditionally. This maxim applies particularly to those not interested in connecting with you. Treat each one like they mean the world to you. Never express or show favorites.
- Spend time and get to know grandchildren individually or in small groups. Although it is wonderful to have entire family get-togethers, the kids generally do not spend time with grandparents if cousins are available.
- Go to grandchildren's sporting, music, or other events as often as possible.

One mother had a teenage daughter who was learning to play tetherball (a ball attached to a rope which hangs from the top of a pole). The girl asked her mother to come outside to help her practice.

"What would you like me to do?" asked the mother.

"Just watch," the girl replied, "and when I am done say, 'Good job. Good job.'"

What is the role of grandparents at a grandchild's event? Just watch, and when the event is done say, "Good job. Good job."

Gift Giving to Grandchildren

Picking the right gifts for grandchildren can be a little challenging.

Here are some thoughts:
- Do not overshadow what the parents are giving.
- Try to know grandkids well enough to know their likes and passions. Kim recently made aprons and tote bags for two young granddaughters for their birthdays. One's favorite snacks are watermelon and seaweed. The other loves cotton candy, cupcakes, and anything sweet. So, Kim made aprons out of material that depicted their preferred snacks. (You ought to try finding material that shows both watermelons and seaweed. Kim settled on watermelons only.)
- Rich's mom was a librarian, so she always gave grandchildren gift cards to bookstores. Her requirement was that they share the book they

chose with her. In this way, Shirley kept up on each grandchild's interests.

- As the grandchildren age, it becomes more difficult to give them anything that they will want or need. So, many grandparents give money. But even gifts of money can take many forms. We started giving the older kids "themed" socks (such as sports teams or cartoon characters individually chosen for their interests) and money for Christmas and birthdays. They seem to be happy about both the socks and the money. One grandparent gave cash as a gift and put an equal amount into a stock portfolio. Another grandparent sent money and the grandchild's favorite candy for birthdays. One elderly grandmother gave $20 to each grandchild for Christmas. The grandchildren had to purchase their own gift, wrap it, and then open it at a Christmas celebration with her. The child then explained to her why they chose the gift.
- One grandparent took each child out on a "date" for their birthday.
- For Valentine's Day, we give each grandchild an individual valentine in which we both write specific things that we love about that child. We include a gift card to a fast-food restaurant. This combination seems to work for all ages.
- One divorced grandmother with little discretionary income worked all year to personally make a gift for each of her grandchildren for Christmas. Each child cherished those personalized gifts.

Enjoying Elderly Grandparenthood

<u>Younger Grandchildren Visits to Your Home</u>

Make it fun to come to your house. Rich had two sets of grandparents who lived in the same small farming community. He loved all four of them dearly. But the home of one set of grandparents had all kinds of things to entertain children of all ages. The other had almost nothing to occupy grandchildren. Hence, Rich loved to spend time in one home and was anxious to leave the other. A generation later, Rich's mother always kept age-appropriate toys and games for her great-grandchildren. Even her small senior living center apartment contained kid-friendly toys. If children have things with which to play, they will want to come for a visit.

Here are some thoughts to make your home grandchild-friendly for younger children:

- Do different crafts and art projects. Find websites to teach children specific crafts or artwork. Bake cookies together. Provide play dough.
- Go on picnics, hikes, or "adventures." Have a tea party or pirate-themed event.
- Use water guns in the backyard. Create scooter paths with cones on your driveway. Have sidewalk chalk and bubbles available. Create scavenger hunts around the house or neighborhood.
- Allow the smaller grandchildren to make individual fairy gardens. Kim had a large outdoor flowerpot for each grandchild for their own personal garden. The fairy garden houses and figures came from the dollar store, and each child planted the ground

cover. Each spring, they redesigned their new garden.

- Read to them. Let them read to you. Sharing a children's book with a child can be a special experience. Read the same book as one of your grandchildren and then have a book date.
- Celebrate holidays by involving the grandchildren in kid-friendly activities. Paint pumpkins for Halloween. Create homemade valentines. Make Christmas cookies. Set up leprechaun traps for St. Patrick's Day.
- Have a sleepover. Enjoy movie nights with popcorn and treats.
- Share family history stories or make up games about your family's background.
- Play board games or hide and seek with them. Help them build forts out of cushions and sheets. After an afternoon at grandma's home, one young child stopped just before entering his dad's car, threw up his arms, and yelled, "It was awesome. It was so fun." Grandma had simply played with him.

Teenager Visits to Your Home

Teenage grandchildren obviously have different interests than younger children.

Some ideas for making your home enjoyable to teens are:

- Purchase a Ping-Pong table or pool table. Acquire a video game set. Provide a chess or checkers set. Get age-appropriate board games.

- Make foods they like to eat. Let them assist you with the cooking. Give them choices of foods to prepare.
- Have a piano or other instruments available. Have the grandchildren play for you. Or you can play for them.
- Acquire the complete set of Calvin and Hobbes comic strips or other humorous books, which can keep teenagers engaged for hours.
- If you have handiwork hobbies (woodworking, craft making, quilt making), let them participate. If you work on cars, invite them to join you.
- Get compact outdoor games such as bocce, lawn darts, corn hole, or other suitable games for yards of any size.
- Watch TV, sports, or movies together. Record "Battle Bots" (robot fighting) episodes to watch with grandsons.

Great Advice

Years ago, one of the best pieces of advice we received as new parents was, "You cannot raise children while sitting down." That wise statement became an important part of our philosophy when our children were still at home. As grandparents, we do not have the energy we once had. But the counsel still holds true. If you can, get out of your easy chair to interact with grandchildren. You build relationships with children best by moving about with them.

Disciplining

Disciplining grandchildren is an area of potential concern. Let the parents correct their own children when you are with them. Even when you babysit the grandkids or great-grandchildren, handle them like their parents do. A consistent approach avoids creating confusion for the kids. Never "correct" how parents correct their children. If you do not agree with your son or daughter's parenting approach, just bite your tongue and smile. You had your turn. Now let them have theirs.

Long-Distance Grandchildren

If grandchildren live a long distance away, make extra efforts to connect with them.

Some ideas are:
- Call, text, or FaceTime them often. Have them perform, read, or play a game with you on FaceTime.
- Send monthly or holiday packages.
- Spend time in their homes if you can. When Kim went to visit, she always took a "magic suitcase" which included small gifts or treats for each child. Each child looked forward to what was inside.
- Watch school performances presented live or on the Internet. Congratulate each child after the event. Send text messages to their personal phones.

Vacation Invitations

If you are invited to go somewhere on vacation with them, GO (if you still can)!

- Have no hidden agendas. Choose to have very little input into the schedules. You are a guest. It is their vacation.
- Pay your own way.
- Spend time with each grandchild. Do not just sit with the adults.
- If they have an active vacation, you may no longer have the stamina and balance to keep up with them. So, take pictures and participate whenever you can.

Concluding Thoughts about Grandparenting

Grandparenting can be one of the great joys in our latter years. Make a concerted and intentional effort to build relationships and memories. Do not passively wait for your family to reach out to you. Become delightfully old to your posterity.

Five years after Kim's encounter with 5-year-old Bentley, she had a similar episode with another delightful 5-year-old grandson, Danny.

Sitting on her lap, he turned to closely look at her and asked, "Why are you so old?"

She responded, "Because I am 70."

Astonished and not grasping what that meant, he exclaimed, "Seven! You are VERY old for seven!"

And so, yes, Kim is VERY old to five-year-old grandchildren.

Life Beyond 70

Thoughts to ponder:

How can I become a better grandparent?

_____

_____

_____

_____

_____

_____

_____

_____

Chapter 6

Adjusting To Dependency

Kim's mom, in her eighties, ended up in the hospital as she approached the abrupt loss of her independence. Like falling off a cliff, one day Della Mae had her beloved home, her long-time neighbors, her many friends, a lifetime of possessions, and her car. The next day, she was scheduled to move into a senior living center where she knew no one, her possessions would be scattered and disbursed, and her car would be gone. The decline of her health, both physical and mental, had precipitated the needed move to the center. Until that point, she had enjoyed relative independence, lonely from losing her recently deceased husband, but still hanging onto her freedom. Overnight, Della Mae's autonomy was arranged to evaporate. The expected loss of independence triggered a stay in the hospital.

In contrast, Rich's parents experienced the transition to increased dependency relatively smoothly. The key for them was that they chose to move out of their home into an assisted-living condo before they were forced to do so. Parkinson's disease reduced Shirley's ability to perform normal household duties, including cooking. Before moving, Dolan labored as he accepted more and more of her chores. They still had each other. They still had a car. But both were exhausted trying to maintain their independence. So, they sold their home and moved into the condo. For several years, they remained in their condo until their health required the next transition to an apartment in a senior living center. Eventually, Dolan died, and Shirley was left alone. At that point she was comfortably settled into the lifestyle of the center, and she only had to deal with the loss of her husband.

Our parents' transitions exemplify two alternative approaches to the loss of independence. One method delays the change as long as possible. The other strategy involves a gradual shift over an extended period of time. Both types of transitions have their pluses and minuses. Both can work. We are not advocating for one or the other. Each person must decide how they wish to address the conversion.

When we are younger, most of us do not consider that we will eventually lose control over our lives. We take simple choices for granted as if they will always be there. Hence, when the time comes that our decision-making options become restricted, we bemoan the loss of our precious independence.

The point at which our freedom becomes more limited has nothing to do with our age. Some remain independent decades longer than others. Several separate triggers can lead to increased dependency. Deteriorating health can compel adjustments in our lifestyle. A decline in either eyesight or hearing can force us to evolve. The regression of a person's cognitive capabilities is a frequent impetus. Sometimes, the change of a spouse's health is an activation point. Likewise, the death of a husband or wife can trigger the need for more help for the surviving person. Any of these challenges can independently or in combination cause a person to need more assistance to continue a comfortable and safe life.

Frustration over the loss of independence is generally a temporary challenge. Most seniors come to grips with their new circumstances. Acceptance of the new situation is achieved. Life moves on. Good years continue. In order to provide suggestions, we divide the loss of independence into three groups of changes, all three of which most elderly will face:

1. **Transportation Changes**
2. **Residence Changes**
3. **Mindset Changes**

1. Transportation Changes

Driving Vehicles

Americans move about by driving themselves. Except in big cities, public transportation is not our primary mode of getting places. Walking is even less frequently employed to go any kind of distance. And bicycles are primarily recreational. For the most part, Americans drive themselves when they want to get somewhere.

Unfortunately, at some point, every person grows out of their ability to safely drive a vehicle. One senior woman realized she needed to give up driving when, at dusk, she nearly hit a pedestrian walking on the side of the road. She was so rattled by the experience that she vowed never to drive again.

Car-driving privileges are generally subtracted gradually and are often initially removed by the aging person themselves. Night driving usually goes first, followed by the elimination of freeways and fast-moving highways. Many eventually restrict themselves to just driving around town to run errands. Ultimately, everyone needs to completely stop driving. Hopefully, that final step happens before a tragedy occurs.

With each gradual reduction in one's driving privileges, a piece of independence is removed. The final elimination of one's ability to drive immediately creates a dependency upon others to run errands and to take the elderly to appointments and commitments. This dependency also forces a loss of privacy since the older person can no longer go alone to make personal purchases of medicines, clothing articles, or even Depends. The privilege of driving a car is directly connected to our level of independence.

We have a son who lives with his family in New York City. At first, they owned a car. But for the last several years, they only use public transportation except when they rent a car to leave the city. Living in a big city for the elderly, poses a different set of challenges. The hustle and bustle of subways and buses can be overwhelming to the elderly. Some graduate to only using a taxi or an Uber to get around. But the elderly can eventually even get frustrated with the simple risks of getting safely in and out of a taxi. Sooner or later, vehicular transportation becomes a challenge for everyone.

> ### *Thoughts for Caregivers*
> Unfortunately, the aging person may not recognize the need to completely discontinue driving before it becomes obvious to others. One senior friend knocked over her daughter's mailbox a second time when the car keys were retrieved, and the car conveniently drove off with a granddaughter to college. The end of driving is sometimes initiated by either loved ones or by the state authorities. Once Rich's father stopped driving, he kept his car for his "Uber" driver, a grandson, to run errands and to chauffeur him places.

Personal Transportation

The loss of one's driving privileges is disappointing. The eventual inability to safely walk poses an even greater impediment to our independence. Toddlers tumble frequently, but young bodies bounce on the ground generally without much damage. Falling does not work so well for the aged.

Many falls can be avoided. Canes provide a third point of contact with the floor and are the first level of balance improvement. When canes no longer give us enough support, we graduate to walkers. Many elderly refuse to use a walker until after they have fallen at least once. That choice is particularly true when moving short distances within a person's home or apartment. A good percentage of the residents living in senior living centers have some pretty ugly bruises from falling before they start using a walker.

Fortunately, many versions of walkers exist. Some have wheels; others have tennis balls or "sliding feet." Some have seats for emergency sitting which can also be used as a shelf to carry things. Baskets attached to the front of a walker can significantly improve the ability to transport items. Some walkers are tall allowing the user to lean on their arms and not just their hands. Walkers designed to fold up can be a great help in providing needed personal space, particularly in senior living centers where many of the residents use walkers. Check out the walker options before you invest.

Many elderly eventually progress from walkers to wheelchairs. Again, models come in various styles and sizes. Generally, the rider becomes dependent upon someone to push the chair, or the elderly must figure out how to scoot around without help. Either way, once the person is in the chair, the risk of falling is eliminated.

During the last two years of his mother's life, Rich drove 50 miles to her senior living center once a week to take her out for an early dinner. She loved to go to a few restaurants that she and Dolan had enjoyed together. At that point, she could still walk slowly at home with a walker. But her wheelchair worked better in the bustle of a restaurant. Her appetite was not such that she could eat an entire meal, so she liked to take the leftovers home to eat later.

After one enjoyable meal, Rich placed the leftover container on the car's roof as he helped her get into the car and then placed the wheelchair in the trunk. They had a

Adjusting To Dependency

nice chat as they drove the five-mile trip back to her center. Once she was back in the wheelchair, he remembered where he had placed the leftovers. No longer on top of the car, they laughed that the leftovers were now spread along the roadside. The logistics of wheelchairs can be complicated for both the user as well as those who push it.

From push-wheelchairs, the next upgrade in personal transportation is an electric wheelchair. Mobility can dramatically improve through the acquisition of a powered chair. Although expensive, these electric chairs can, under certain circumstances, be funded by government agencies. Most seniors can learn to safely steer an electric wheelchair. But just like the ability to drive a car, one becomes more proficient with practice. Running over others' feet can be painful and is not uncommon. Proficiency in backing up requires effort. Maneuvering in tight spaces is a skill to be mastered. Most seniors, however, can learn how to safely drive a motorized chair.

A resident of a senior living center with a regular wheelchair was frustrated that she was dependent on others to push her around to get to meals and activities. The problem was resolved with the acquisition of an electric wheelchair. The woman was thereafter free to move about independently without requiring the assistance of others.

Kim's dad spent the last four years of his life in a hospital bed, which was set up in the living room of their home. In hindsight, Paul would have enjoyed puttering around in an electric wheelchair. He was coherent. His upper body worked fine. Due to a stroke, his legs would no longer function well. We now recognize that an electric wheelchair would have been a great improvement to the quality of life in his final years.

Rich's dad got an electric wheelchair when he was in his late eighties. Dolan initially ignored that there were two speed settings on the machine. He raced down the halls of their senior living center, leaving Shirley with her walker in the dust. Eventually, they figured out how to travel at the same speed.

2. **Residence Changes**

Moving

A person's loss of independence is often triggered by a change in their long-time residence. Residing in one's home, either alone or with a spouse, provides a level of control that disappears once the person relocates to some form of assisted living. Later in this chapter, we will review some options for the elderly to obtain the needed assistance while remaining in their existing residence. But let us first review what happens when forced to move. Although the elderly understand that they are moving, the implications of that transition are rarely fully anticipated. Becoming dependent is tough. Losing your long-time residence is part of why the transition to dependency is so difficult.

A separate loss occurs when the individual must get rid of their "stuff." If a person has lived in the same house for decades, they have grown accustomed to the furniture, decorations, clothing, and even their lawn mower. Letting go of one's treasures is hard. In her 70s, Kim's mother was still storing her maternity clothes. The home itself can be a

Adjusting To Dependency

beloved location of cherished memories. Downsizing is difficult; severely downsizing to fit into a much smaller new residence can be traumatizing.

> ### *Thoughts for Caregivers*
> Caregivers' compassion during a move is most helpful to the displaced person. Leaving one's long-time residence is a huge emotional challenge. Even if the person seems prepared to make the move before it begins, once ties to the former residence are cut, the elderly often initially wish they had not made the move. A caregiver's anticipation of this emotional event can help the elderly adjust.

When Rich's parents moved into their assisted-living condo, Shirley insisted on keeping all her spare furniture, furnishings, and accumulated objects that did not fit into their living space. Almost nothing was given away or discarded. Even never-used sleeping bags, which they had purchased decades earlier, were retained even though she and Dolan had never been campers. Initially, everything was stacked, Tetris-style, into the condo's basement. When they moved to an apartment, the huge pile of extra things got restacked into a large storage unit. Although she never even saw the storage unit, it was maintained until she died. Even if she had visited the unit, she could have had no access to anything packed inside. For some, having "theoretical access" to one's mementos can be helpful, even if "true access" is not a reality. Our "stuff" can be very important to us.

> ### *Thoughts for Caregivers*
> Having a say in what is discarded can help the elderly's adjustment. Each article for consideration, however, has corresponding memories. Hence, the decision-making process can be agonizingly slow for those who are assisting. Schedule enough time to not force the elderly to "rush" the process. Sometimes, several stages are needed to complete the process of cleaning out "treasures."

While decisions to dispose of a lifetime of gathered assets are difficult, moving can also have a positive "freeing" effect on the person leaving. Home management responsibilities including appliance repairs, plumbing challenges, walls that need painting, a leaky roof, and the constant upkeep of a yard are all thankfully removed. Buying groceries and cooking duties are also eliminated. While saddened by the loss of certain freedoms, the daily worries of managing one's own home disappear.

> ### *Thoughts for Caregivers*
> When is the right time for an elderly person to end living independently? When should one consider moving to some form of assisted living? This decision is one that most seniors want to delay as long as possible. Consequently, many wait until they are encouraged by their loved ones to make the move. Here are some signs that the time might be right for the elderly to consider a more assisted living arrangement:
> * Safety becomes an issue.
> * The caregiving spouse or partner is exhausted.

Adjusting To Dependency

> * Health challenges intensify or weight changes are occurring.
> * Loss of memory becomes evident, possibly including confused wandering.
> * The individual can no longer safely drive.
> * Home maintenance becomes a challenge.
> * Companionship becomes a greater need.
> * Bills are not getting paid, or expenses are overwhelming the budget.
> * Families, living elsewhere, are taking care of most needs.

Residence Options

Several residence options exist for addressing the incremental support needs of the elderly. Some of the alternatives allow the elderly to continue living in their current residence.

Some options are:
- A live-in caregiver is an approach that permits the person to remain in their home. Various financial arrangements are possible including simply providing room and board for the caregiver or the caregiver's family. Different levels of care are also available. An outside-the-home caregiver who comes in regularly is also feasible.
- Getting married or taking on a live-in partner may address the dependency needs of the elderly who are currently living alone. This decision includes a choice regarding where to live including the possibility of remaining in the person's current

home. The topic of marriage is addressed in a later chapter.

- Downsizing from a larger home to a smaller home can sometimes reduce the upkeep requirements of a more spacious house. Moving to a condo or home where a homeowners' association takes care of the yard, outside structural maintenance, and snow removal can also reduce the day-to-day pressure as one ages.
- The home of a son or daughter is a frequent residence selection. Sometimes this takes the form of a single room. Other times a basement is free. If the home has a separate kitchen, that can add a level of independence.

Moving in with one's family creates its own set of challenges. All involved must recognize that such a move in no way resembles the status quo when the elderly lived independently. The elderly visitor is not coming for a temporary stay. The family has a lifestyle rhythm that will require some adjustment. The elderly must adapt to being a long-term guest. Acclimatizing to a new schedule, new lifestyle, and new food is required.

Some people are very particular about how they want their food prepared. We have had a couple of short-term guests in our home that would be extremely difficult to have as permanent or even semi-permanent residents. One elderly friend stayed only two days with us before moving into her daughter's home in another state. At the end of her

Adjusting To Dependency

short visit in our home, we could see how difficult this new arrangement was going to be, for the elderly friend as well as for her daughter's family.

If you become the permanent houseguest of your family members, be prepared for many changes. Become a welcome houseguest. Consider the host's needs, as well as your own.

- One doctor built a small home with a living area/kitchen, bedroom, and bath in his backyard for his 85-year-old mother-in-law. She loved her independence. But she could quickly access help if needed. The backyard also housed two huge Great Danes who liked to nuzzle her when she came outside. Fearing the dogs would knock her over, she solved the problem by carrying a three-wood golf club to bonk the dogs on the head if they became too friendly.
- A non-family-member caregiver's home is also a possibility. Kim's mom stayed with a former daughter-in-law who was a retired hospice nurse for the last year of her life.
- Retirement or age-restricted communities allow a significant level of independence while possibly providing some basic services like housecleaning, laundry, and transportation.
- An assisted living supported condo can provide additional levels of service, including meals, activities, and medical support.
- Apartments within a senior living facility are an option. The size of the apartment and services

provided vary greatly from one facility to another. Corresponding costs can be significantly different as well.

If financially an option, senior living centers have many benefits for both the elderly as well as for their family members. Most residents of assisted living facilities prefer to be in the center versus staying with their family members. One obvious benefit is the social aspects of making many new friends who are experiencing the same life challenges that they are.

- Nursing homes provide continuous, 24-hour care for chronically ill people and resemble a hospital setting.

Thoughts for Caregivers

Many family members feel guilty if their elderly parent(s) is moved to a senior living center, but they need not feel that way. The lifestyle in a center has many advantages over living in a family member's home.

* The center provides friends and activities.
* The social network is far greater than a family can provide.
* The elderly are not relying on their family members to entertain them.
* The caregiver's family keeps its independence.
* Emergency medical attention is available onsite.

Adjusting To Dependency

Senior Living Center Considerations

Most regions of the country have multiple senior living centers from which to choose. Researching the various options can be done online. Another approach is to use a "broker" to provide useful comparisons between the options in the area. These brokers are compensated through a commission paid by the facility (at no cost to the potential resident.) Of course, onsite visits are needed to finalize which one to choose.

Here are some things to consider:

- **Vacancy.** Availability or the lack thereof reflects either the supply of senior living center options in the area or the relative quality of a particular facility. Some centers have a waiting list, secured by a deposit, to get into the facility at all or for the more desirable units within the facility.
- **Cost.** Understand what is included in the monthly fees. Historically, how often have rent increases been implemented, and when is the next anticipated?
- **Medical support and safety.** Each center has different levels of services with corresponding costs. Are in-house CNAs (certified nursing assistants) and access to home-visit doctors provided? Does the facility offer call buttons to access medical support? Managing medications is a feature to be understood. On-site podiatry care and nail services can be desirable.

- **Activities provided by the center.** Review the daily, weekly, and/or monthly calendar of events to understand what activities are provided.
- **Activities provided by external sources.** Are church services provided in the center? What other externally generated activities are available?
- **Activities for family members.** Events for family members can be sponsored, including those for grandchildren.
- **Types of facility.** Different facilities have different areas of focus, such as regular living versus a memory center versus a rehab center. Be sure your needs are matched to the right kind of facility. The residents, who represent potential new friends, reflect the type of center they live in.
- **Size of the facility.** The larger the facility, the more activities and support levels are generally available.
- **Culture of the facility.** Some facilities can be friendlier than others. Get a feel for the underlying culture.
- **Geographic distance from external caregivers.** If the facility is too far from where family members reside, their visits will be less frequent.
- **Food – meals and available treats.** The quality of the food is an important consideration. Wait times to be served also affect the meal experiences. Having a 24-hour self-serve "bistro" with various snacks, soft drinks, and juice available can be helpful.

- **Food preparation options available within resident apartments.** A small kitchen in the apartment can help to bridge the needs when a resident is in a hurry or just wants to fix their own meal.
- **Amenities.** In-house facilities, such as hairdressing/barbers, exercise facilities, and physical therapy support, allow residents to remain in the facility to access desired services.
- **Cars.** Some facilities require that residents give up their cars.
- **Transportation.** Does the facility provide transportation to doctor appointments and shopping trips?

Adjusting to the corresponding loss of independence can be mitigated somewhat by the pleasantness of the facility. The opposite can also be true. Do your homework about alternatives. And expect an adjustment period.

3. Mindset Adjustments

The loss of independence is a challenging mental adjustment. Nobody chooses to grow old. Nobody wants to become dependent. But eventually, most must learn to adjust to some form of assisted living. For instance, if one enters a senior living center, they miss their home. They miss their neighbors and friends. They certainly miss their car if it disappeared in the move. They must make new friends, which they may not have had to do in decades. But mostly, they struggle with the sudden loss of simple choices they were previously free to make. Whether the loss of independence happens as the elderly enter a senior living facility or through some other residential option, adjusting their attitude to this change of circumstances is the only path to cope with the transition. Assisted living, no matter where you live, is simply different than unassisted living.

Here are some suggestions to help to mentally deal with the loss of independence:

- Some believe that their loss of independence could have been avoided. They focus on what they could have done differently. Or they are annoyed with their children who were encouraging that changes be made. Unfortunately, losing your independence eventually happens to all who are aging. Adjusting to your new circumstances is the best course of action now. It is time to move on.
- Be pleasant company. Ask others about themselves. Be interested in their families. Become a good listener. It is easy to focus every conversation on yourself or your health. Stay curious about others. One senior at a family reunion simply turned to a college-age granddaughter whom she had not seen for quite some time and said, "Tell me about your life," and then listened attentively.
- Enjoy the scenery that whoever is driving you around cannot observe. We recently visited our daughter in Boston. Unfortunately, she got COVID as we arrived, and we were on our own for a week to explore the sites in the area. On the day we were to fly home, she felt well enough to take us to the

Adjusting To Dependency

airport, but she asked that Rich drive the forty-five-minute trip to get there. At one point as we moved through the traffic, she reflected that she was enjoying seeing the sights that she normally never noticed when she was driving. Passengers have a different perspective than the driver.

- Retain your sense of humor. One resident of a senior living center was so loving, kind, and humorous that the CNAs (nurses) cried when he passed away. As the saying goes, honey goes further than vinegar when asking for help.
- Sometimes, a person compensates for the loss of independence by becoming demanding. Be interested in those who serve you. Be nice. Be grateful to those who help.

Rich's dad was normally a kind and caring person. In his later years, his demeanor changed, however, whenever he went to a restaurant. Inexplicably, in that one environment, Dolan became more demanding and less flexible. He failed to recognize the change from his normally pleasant behavior.

One of the challenges of getting old is that cooking duties eventually fall to others. When living in someone's home or in a senior living center, you cannot control or even influence what food is placed before you. Do not become whiney. Nobody enjoys being with somebody who constantly complains about the food prepared for them. At restaurants, be kind to those waiting on you. They are not the chefs. Becoming delightfully old does not include becoming an angry food critic.

Dining rooms in senior living centers are somewhat like a restaurant with two exceptions. First, the same people show up to eat three meals a day. Second, the patrons have frequent interactions with the chef. After a lifetime of fixing meals to their own liking, dining halls require a transition in thinking. Seniors, by nature, can be particular about their eating preferences. Any cafeteria chef is going to be challenged to meet the diverse needs of all or even most of the residents. Chefs in these facilities tend to turn over frequently because of the cumulative impact of the resident complaints. We do not have an answer for this conundrum. But constant complaining seems to make the problem worse.

Family members who take in an elderly parent might face the same criticism about food, except there would be one complainer instead of many. A loss of independence includes a loss of cooking duties as well. Each home chef prepares food differently. The permanent houseguest's palate must adjust to accommodate those to whom cooking duties now fall. One family, with a highly demanding senior parent, mitigated some of her complaints by assigning her one meal a week to prepare her "signature" enchiladas.

- One mindset challenge is that our historical identity can feel threatened by the transition to becoming dependent. In the opening story of this chapter, we outlined how difficult it was for Della Mae to move to a senior living center. Her response, however, was not abnormal for a person who has been prominent in their long-time community. Losing a circle of adoring supporters who revere your life of achievements can be devastating. Moving to a senior living center where few, if any, know of your history can be hard on your self-esteem. The loss of your independence can be rough. An attack on your identity can add to the challenge. A positive mindset towards this new normal is the first step to a successful adjustment.

- Look for resources to help with your needs. For instance, home deliveries of medicines, groceries, and meals can help. We are amazed at the number of things that can be ordered from Amazon, grocery stores, and pharmacies that are delivered in mere hours and at no additional cost.

One couple that moved into a senior living center was immediately delighted to be there. Even though they dealt with all the changes inherent to this transition, including selling their home, eliminating their household possessions, and leaving their neighbors and friends, their attitudes were so positive that they immediately loved their new residence. Their motivation for moving was simply looking ahead at expected health changes in the coming years. The husband had a treatable cancer, and both were in their mid-eighties. They immediately started making new friends and participated in all the activities that the center had to offer. Hence, their transition time to the loss of their independence was zero. Of course, it helped that they could still drive. But due to their choice to have a positive attitude, even the eventual loss of their car did not unduly set them back.

We wish we could avoid losing our independence. But part of life is aging. And part of aging is the loss of personal freedoms. This change in our lifestyle circumstances can be a rough transition. While difficult, adjusting to this new normal can be positively accomplished. Much good still lies ahead. Let us move forward with optimism.

Thoughts for Caregivers

Caregivers can positively contribute to the adjustment process of someone losing their independence. First, recognize that this transition is happening. Be willing to listen to the vetting of frustrations. Those making the adjustment are often surprised by their new circumstances. They need to verbalize what is happening to sort it out in their own minds. Just listen with patience and compassion.

Thoughts to ponder:

What is my plan to transition to dependency?

_____

_____

_____

Adjusting To Dependency

Chapter 7

Addressing Loneliness

Being elderly and alone does not always lead to a state of loneliness. We can be proactive in filling our lives with people and activities that bring us joy, peace, friendships, and satisfaction.

We have a grandson, Simon, who is an excellent distance runner. The longer the distance, the more he enjoys the race. When Simon was in the seventh grade, he signed up to compete in the steeplechase event at the state track meet. He had never run that race before, and in fact, he had never even seen a steeplechase. The race differs from other distance races because it has a series of fixed hurdles runners must jump over along the 2,000-meter race. One of the barriers has a pool of water in which to land. To prepare, Simon got on the Internet and studied strategies for running this race. On the first day of the track meet, he ran the 1600, which is just short of a mile. He placed on the podium putting him with the top runners in the state. The steeplechase was scheduled on the second day of the track meet, and he looked forward to the challenge of the barriers and the longer distance.

On the day of the race, to his surprise, no one else had signed up for the steeplechase in his age group. Undaunted, Simon lined up alone and waited for the starter's gun. Off he went at what he thought was a good pace. After a couple of laps, others at the meet noticed that he was running alone. At first, there were a few encouraging shouts to him as he circled the track and leaped over the barriers. As the race progressed, more of the crowd picked up on what was happening. Simon is a delightfully gregarious kid, so some in the crowd knew his name. Before long, many at the event were calling out to him. He finished the race with the best kick he could muster and raised both hands as he broke the tape. The crowd clapped its approval as the new state steeplechase champion beamed. Simon then made his way to the podium where he stood alone at the top to receive his first-place medal. What could have been a lonely endeavor became positive through the support of the crowd.

As we become elderly, we sometimes feel like we are running alone the steeplechase of life. As we negotiate the barriers of the aging process, we can feel there are few spectators to cheer us. We generally start our lives with our direct family members. Parents, siblings, and grandparents are part of our original group of close associates. As we attend school, we add peer-group friends. In college and/or at work, we expand our circle of acquaintances. If we marry, our relationships dramatically change with a spouse and potentially our own children becoming our primary life companions. Ultimately, the quantity of our associations begins to recede as children leave home, and we eventually retire. The decline of our friend-circle continues as our grandparents, parents, and siblings pass away. Over time, we lose contact with many of our friends and acquaintances. A divorce can exacerbate our isolation. A child that precedes us in death is particularly difficult. These losses collectively contribute to our feelings of loneliness.

The loss of a cherished spouse or partner is often the most dramatic change in our friend base. Losing the association of an almost constant companion is a major challenge. We think about them frequently. We miss doing simple things together, like running an errand or watching a TV show or movie. Meals are not the same. We covet that relationship when it is no longer available. One disappointed senior lost his wife when they were both 93. He later confided that her death was the hardest thing that had ever happened to him.

Retiring from the workforce can also be a trigger for loneliness. If we worked, socialized, and had lunch with co-workers, vendors, and customers, the solitude of retirement can hit us like a freight train. Teachers, for instance, have human interactions in classrooms, with fellow teachers, and even with parents. All these relationships end with retirement. And if retirement is combined with the loss of a spouse, we can really feel lost.

Loneliness is a strong emotion that can happen anywhere and at any time. The feeling is complex with various degrees of intensity. We forlornly miss those who once were with us. We long for times gone by. Memories can unexpectedly be triggered by sights, sounds, or even smells. We can feel lonely when surrounded by a crowd, even if that crowd is made up of younger members of our own family. Conversely, just being alone does not necessarily cause us to feel lonely. So, given the abstract nature of deep loneliness, let us review some practical solutions to loneliness.

These suggestions are grouped into six overlapping categories:
1. **Time**
2. **Increasing Connections**
3. **Service**
4. **Solo Activities**
5. **Senior Living Centers**
6. **Getting Married**

1. <u>Time</u>

Mourning the loss of any loved one takes time. If that loved one is a beloved spouse or partner both the duration as well as the magnitude of our grief can be greater. Time gives us distance to adjust to the way grief may be part of our lives. As the days go by, we gradually adapt to our new circumstances. For each person, the length of time necessary for our sorrow to subside is different. Some can reconcile relatively quickly. Others never totally get over their loss. Time works best in combination with the other solutions outlined in this chapter. If we rely solely on the passage of time, our period of loneliness may extend longer.

2. **Increasing Connections**

Living alone can be lonely. Moving into the home of a son or daughter can help, but the busy lives of those with whom we stay do not always match up with our need for associations. So, we must seek external connections beyond our living space.

Here are some activities that could expand and strengthen our social network:

- Getting out of the house, even to the grocery store, can be a welcome change of perspective. Seek to become friendly with those you see regularly at Starbucks, gas stations, and grocery stores. Use their nametags to greet them by name. Most customers come and go without much interaction. Find a way to make their jobs more enjoyable.
- Making telephone and FaceTime calls reduces loneliness. Distance no longer matters since we can virtually connect anywhere in the world with family and friends. Reach out to those who no longer live close by or to those who are also isolated. Do not wait for others to call you. Make a list of everyone you can call. Start with brief five minutes calls to gradually build a telephone relationship. You might start by setting a daily alarm at 10 a.m. When the alarm goes off, call a friend, a family member, or an acquaintance in a hospital or rehab center.

  Rich had a close friend who died of pancreatic cancer. For his friend's last eight months, Rich spoke to him on the phone every day for 10 to 30 minutes. These calls were therapeutic for both Rich and his friend, and certainly helped his friend feel less isolated. Even though he lived nearby, the man preferred phone calls to personal visits, which would have required him to spruce up. Interestingly, the calls also served an unexpected purpose. His daughters and his sister took turns living with him during those months. At his funeral, these women expressed their appreciation for Rich's phone calls. The friend only revealed how he was truly feeling to Rich. So, the daughters and sister listened quietly from the next room to get a daily update about his evolving health condition.

- Organize a "lunch bunch" with friends in similar circumstances. Set up a bridge group or sponsor Bunco sessions. Join or organize a book club. Local libraries often have book groups.
- Go for a daily walk with a friend. Even if you need a walker, get out and move around.
- Attending church services can help. One elderly widow became an amazing greeter in her congregation. Families of all ages became her dear friends as she welcomed newcomers into the congregation. Her favorable impact was so appreciated that one family even named their newborn baby "Genevieve" in her honor.
- Locate the community center for seniors, which may provide organized activities such as exercise groups or craft-building/art opportunities.

Addressing Loneliness

- One widow joined other single women who wanted to travel. Choosing and planning the excursion was part of the experience. Annually, they took cruises or joined guided tour groups.
- Attend classes at a community college or community center. Pick out something interesting. Who cares about grades? Audit a class. Just learn something new. Many community colleges offer discounts to seniors.
- Grandchildren's performances can either be attended in person or be viewed virtually. Either way, follow up with the child after the event to congratulate them on their efforts.
- Both Rich's mother and our oldest daughter lived alone. Although they were 2,000 miles apart, they simultaneously watched Hallmark movies while conversing on the phone. This same daughter and Rich also watched televised NBA basketball games together while telephoning each other. The only problem was that her TV feed was delayed a few seconds. Hence, he reacted to a great play seconds before she could see it. You do not have to be in the same room with somebody to enjoy watching something together.

3. <u>Service</u>

When lonely, we become inwardly focused. Seeking ways to serve others can expand our attention beyond ourselves.

Some ideas for service may include:
- Volunteer at a food bank, school, homeless shelter, museum, refugee organization, or woman's shelter. Become a driver for Meals on Wheels or for a food pantry.
- Read to someone who has eyesight issues. Senior living centers have many residents with macular degeneration who might appreciate someone reading to them.
- Knit or loom beanies for a community center or newborns. Sew quilts for women/children's shelters. One widow organized a day of service every week for others like her to make things to give away.
- Make toys for less fortunate children. One elderly man formed a group that made small wooden toy cars for refugee and homeless children.
- Seek to do random acts of kindness for friends, family, waitresses, nurses, cashiers, neighbors, and children. A goal of one small act each day can mitigate our lonely feelings.
- Set aside the first day of every month to write a brief letter or email to somebody.

4. **Solo Activities**

Being alone does not necessarily cause us to be lonely. New hobbies can enhance the time we spend by ourselves.

Addressing Loneliness

Some solo activities to consider might be:

- Get a pet. Interactive pets, like dogs and cats, can be therapeutic for the elderly. A high-maintenance pet might just be what is needed. In addition, walking a dog gets you outside and can provide interactions with others who love dogs.
- Write a short story or even the novel that has been stuck in your head. One senior wrote a new poem each day.
- Take up painting. Many seniors find creating artwork to be energizing. Classes, either online or in person, can help to refine your talent. Both George Bush and Dwight Eisenhower became artists when their White House years were over.
- Knitting, crocheting, or quilting are solo activities that work for some aging people.
- Woodworking can be enjoyable. One man became proficient at making custom-designed wooden writing pens, which he gave as gifts.
- Building model trains or cars from kits or Legos can be enjoyable. A man in his nineties regularly received gifts of detailed model kits from his family to keep him busy.
- Memorize things. One senior woman gathered jokes, which she constantly shared with everyone she met. Commit to memory a poem or scripture passage each day.
- Learn to play an instrument or revive an old skill. Rich's mother started taking piano lessons in her elderly years. One aging piano teacher could no

longer read the notes on sheet music. She then discovered a new ability, playing the piano by ear.
- Sing or hum to yourself. Find songs from a favorite group or big band and put to memory the lyrics. Or learn the words to favorite hymns.

5. **Senior Living Centers**

One of the primary benefits of a senior living center is social. Having many people around you who are also elderly creates opportunities to make interpersonal connections. The impetus for moving to a center is generally the growing inability to care for yourself. So, while solving that problem, the center can also successfully address loneliness as well.

Ideas for being pro-active in a senior living center might include:
- Participate in the center-sponsored activities.
- Open your door. One elderly woman so embraced the thought of making new friends that she kept her door open in her senior living center during the daytime. She, thereby, invited all who passed by to come in and be with her. This open-door approach was a blessing to her and to the many that enjoyed her company.
- Create your own activities. Seniors should not feel limited to just the activities that the center sponsors. One group of men and women organized their own "poker group" playing for small amounts of money. Another woman set up games of Rummikub every afternoon. Inviting others to join in working on

puzzles can help. One group organized a billiards tournament every Saturday morning. Seek out those who are just as lonely as you are.

6. **Getting Married**

This topic is covered in the next chapter.

Loneliness can impact us at any point in the aging process. If we do not yet need caregiver support, seek solutions to constructively fill your time and to build your friend base. If you have caregivers involved in your life, seek answers that go beyond what your current support group can provide. Caregivers are busy. The elderly must allow these helpers to have balance in their lives. Whatever your stage in life, be proactive about finding your own keys to tackling loneliness.

Thoughts to ponder:

How do I want to address loneliness?

_____

_____

_____

_____

Life Beyond 70

Chapter 8

Marriage At My Age?

Before we discuss marriage between elderly partners, let us make two observations. These opinions are not based on any empirical evidence but on our own experiences.

Our first observation is that with each passing decade of life, the probability that a single senior will marry decreases in likelihood. Many single seniors have figured out how to effectively deal with loneliness without getting married. Sometimes, their first spouse died. Or a divorce may have caused them to be single. Or maybe they never married when they were younger. Whatever the reason for their current unmarried status, they may see no need to marry now. Since women have longer life expectancies than men, the imbalance between the sexes is a partial explanation for the number of senior women who remain single. But we observe that the older a single person is, whether female or male, the less likely they will marry.

Our second observation is that marriages created when individuals are elderly are more likely to flourish than to fail. Seniors that choose to marry often use their life's experiences, both positive and negative, to build a happy union with their new marriage partner. Our conclusion is that most marriages created late in life seem to do well.

Some seniors choose to pair up without ever marrying each other. Having a boyfriend or girlfriend as we age can sometimes make more sense than getting married. The details of that relationship can take many forms. But maintaining a friendship without marrying can be an option.

Just like marriages between people of any age, senior marriages can also fail. One of our friends got remarried late in life. He was a dashing college football player in his youth who rode a motorcycle until his later years. Still handsome and fun, he appeared to be younger than he was. In his 80s, he met and quickly married a beautiful senior-age woman who fell in love with the person that he used to be. Once she discovered that his Parkinson's disease severely limited his activity level, she wanted nothing to do with him.

While failed marriages occur among people of all ages, the factors that affect senior marriages are different from those facing younger people. Here are some things to consider and address when the elderly are contemplating marriage.

Health

If one of the partners has failing health, the marriage quickly becomes a full-time caregiving effort. Even if both elderly parties are healthy the day they marry, at some point in the not-too-distant future, one or both will probably experience health problems. Are both individuals prepared to become the primary caregiver for an elderly person with ill health?

Caregiving for a spouse, either for the first one or for a marriage partner added later in life, is usually a positive experience. Caregiving for a partner can be fulfilling. Frequently, a spouse who cared for their mate for an extended period of time misses the person as well as the caregiving effort when their spouse passes away.

Finances

An approximate equal financial footing takes money out of the equation. But if one party has significantly more finances than the other, lifestyle differences need to be discussed and sorted out. A prenuptial agreement may address financial differences.

We know one woman that remarried quickly twice when each of her first two husbands passed away. As crass as it may sound, she needed money. She simply did not have the resources to provide for her basic needs, and she was open about her financial situation when she dated. Fortunately, she had a delightful personality, was attractive, and enjoyed good health. She made a welcome marriage partner to both her second and third husbands who were actively seeking marriage companionships. While financial motivations were certainly part of her considerations, she became a positive contributor to the lives of each or her husbands.

Discuss who is going to pay for what. Those decisions should be worked out before marriage. Everyday expenses such as food, home repairs, utilities, and insurance should be addressed. Discretionary purchases also need to be discussed. For instance, who is going to pay for vacations and cars and grandchild gifts? Are financial resources going to be comingled or retained separately?

How will inheritances of both families be addressed? Do wills need to change? What happens financially to the remaining spouse if the other spouse dies?

Also, look at income sources that may change due to a marriage. Sometimes, insurance or retirement payments for a deceased spouse are eliminated if the living spouse remarries.

Children

Marriage brings two families together with all the complications of bridging these two groups. Can it work? Yes, absolutely. Can it have difficulties? Yes, absolutely. While late-life marriages can blend two families together, some families choose to remain separate. One excellent senior marriage lasted for fifteen wonderful years until the husband passed away. During that period, the two extended families saw each other exactly twice, at the wedding and at the funeral.

Listen to the concerns of your children. While outsiders generally do not have a complete picture of a couple's relationship, they may see some areas of concern more clearly than you do.

> ### *Thoughts for Caregivers*
> Many couples are not open to suggestions about marriage plans. As hard as it may be, you also want to maintain a positive relationship with the elderly who are considering marriage. If input is requested, choose your words carefully. If your opinion is clearly not wanted, you might want to bite your tongue.
>
> If one of the potential marriage partners suffers from dementia, however, you must question whether the afflicted party can really make good decisions about getting married. Caregivers may, in this case, want to more forcefully make their concerns known.

Where to live?

Choosing where to live is not a trivial decision. Can the two parties work together to choose a space that will be supportive of their new relationship? Financial considerations may dictate the answer. But working this out together prior to the marriage can signal how the two are going to function together.

Sometimes, moving to neutral ground can help the marriage start with a fresh beginning. Relocating to a different house or condo, a senior community, or a senior living center can work. Can the marriage succeed if the new partner moves into the long-time home of the other? Sure. Discuss how this arrangement is going to allow for the two to become equal partners, even though one party enters the space belonging to the other.

Moving towards or away from one spouse's family can alter the dynamics of a senior marriage. Rich's grandfather quickly remarried someone in his small town when his first wife passed away. The mismatch of this couple was immediately evident resulting in a quick divorce. Embarrassed about the outcome, he then quickly married again to another woman who lived 700 miles away. Looking back, since these were pre-internet days, we cannot imagine how he met, let alone got to know her. Once married, he moved to her city, thereby disconnecting himself from his family and long-time friends. The second marriage seemed to the extended family to also be a poor fit. But the union lasted nine years before he passed away. While the true status of how he felt about the marriage is unknown, his marital decision removed him from close contact with his historical support system.

One remarriage of two seniors was strong but encountered unique challenges as they aged. The husband developed dementia, and the wife was no longer capable of taking care of herself or him. Their two families helped to make the decision to sell her home where the couple was living. She then moved into a senior living center, and he moved into the home of one of his children. Once apart, they infrequently saw each other. If this had been their original marriage, they probably would have handled things differently.

Common Interests

Like marriages of younger people, common interests of the two parties are critical to a happy marriage. For the elderly, age cannot be the only thing they have in common. What does each person like to do? At this stage of life, the marriage partners have a lot of time to spend together. Before entering a marriage, take sufficient time to understand what the two of you are going to do together.

Some late-life marriages involve partners that are not similar in age. Just like parties of similar age, the partners need to find common interests.

Compromises
Seniors can be less flexible in their decision making than when they were younger. Many decisions will arise, some critical and some mundane, to which both parties will need to agree. Where to live? Where to vacation? Where to spend holidays? How to spend money? What to have for lunch? Successful marriages are generally built upon compromises.

Courting Duration
Just because you feel you do not have a lot of time left in life does not mean that marriage plans should be rushed. Date each other. Do things together. Take your time to make this work.

Mourning Period
After a person's spouse passes, some choose to remarry quickly while others wait decades. Allow sufficient time to mourn the loss of the deceased spouse. That duration differs for each person. The emotions of the mourning process can distort one's feelings and assessment of a new potential spouse.

Sexual Relations

Just like younger marriages, sexual intimacy is part of the marriage considerations. Talk openly about your expectations and concerns. Seek advice from medical professionals if needed. Figure out what works for both of you.

Predatory Behavior

Occasionally, widows and/or widowers can become stalkers in their desire to quickly find a new spouse. One elderly man proposed to a woman who was about his age. She declined. In less than two weeks, he was engaged to someone else. Beware!

Romance Scams

Unfortunately, romance scams happen and can be difficult to detect. The emotions of a new relationship can obscure good judgment. If you become interested in someone that was previously unknown to you or to others whom you trust, have someone do a background check on them. An online search is simple to do and can remain private. It is better to confirm your positive feelings about the person you like than to be sorry later.

Marriage of two elderly people can be a fulfilling relationship. But, just like when you were young, be careful to not marry too quickly. Have courtship talks about everything. Try to see each other in new or hard situations. Do not be in a rush.

Thoughts for Caregivers

The elderly are usually not capable of doing an online search on someone. They may not even want you to do the search. In today's world, information is readily available on most people. Social media accounts can be particularly revealing. Your efforts to understand an elderly person's new love interest may save them a lot of heartache and/or heartburn.

Thoughts to ponder:

What are my thoughts on getting married?

_____

_____

_____

_____

_____

_____

_____

_____

_____

Life Beyond 70

Chapter 9

Dispelling Worries

A friend of ours who was in her eighties became distraught over the latest military conflict between two distant peoples. She feared that the current battle would morph into the Biblical Armageddon, which would eventually encompass the entire world. With two grandsons in the U.S. Army, she was consumed with the idea that they would soon find themselves fighting the ultimate war. Her fears overwhelmed her normal daily activities. With some counseling, she gradually found ways to overcome her excessive worries.

Once elderly, we can take fears and worries to a much higher intensity than when we were younger. As our capabilities diminish, our ability to deal with everyday challenges can add to the stress. Some of our anxieties can be valid. But others are simply potential problems that have a low probability of affecting us personally. And many

apprehensions are beyond our control or even influence. These worries will be grouped into four general areas.
1. Money
2. Family
3. News
4. Scams

1. Money

If money is not a personal concern for you, you can skip this section. But if your financial situation has you worried, let us provide some suggestions. For any number of reasons, seniors can run out of money before their time runs out. The stress associated with this dilemma is palpable. This problem, however, is neither unusual nor unique. Should this be your challenge, you are still worthwhile. Keep breathing. Let us figure this out.

This section is not a sophisticated review of tax-effective financial strategies. Instead, let us focus on relatively simple solutions if a money shortage is a concern. There are three sides to money:

A. **Money in hand (Savings, investments, assets, etc.)**
B. **Money coming in (income)**
C. **Money going out (expenses)**

A. Money in Hand (Savings, investments, assets)

Since most elderly are retired, the money going out often exceeds the money coming in. The money in hand must,

Dispelling Worries

therefore, make up the difference. Savings and investments, which may have been stockpiled over a lifetime for this very purpose, are the first line of solutions. For many, the concern is that the savings are too small to cover the needs for the uncertain duration of our lives. Calculating how long these assets will last may require some outside assistance.

Beyond financial savings, physical assets are the next line of potential solutions. If we own a home, it often represents our most valuable asset. Eventually, once living independently is no longer prudent, our home can be used to fund some or the entire cash flow shortfall. For instance, many people fund their senior living center expenses through the sale of their home. Or simply downsizing into a smaller home may allow you to meet your personal needs.

A variation on selling your home is a reverse mortgage, which is a loan against your home's equity. If the homeowner is at least 62 years old, no monthly payments may be required. The homeowner must remain living in the home and the loan is repaid at death, the sale of the home, or if the owner permanently moves out. Do your homework about requirements and details of these loans before you decide to go this route.

If you own whole-life insurance, it is possible to borrow from the policy's cash value or receive part of the policy's face value as a loan. Check with your insurance provider if you want to consider this option.

Selling a boat, an RV, or a second automobile also represents possibilities. Eventually, you may not even need one car, let alone two. Selling some personal items like jewelry or a piano might help as well. The problem is when the money in hand is dwindling too quickly. What other options can we pursue?

B. Money Coming In (Income)

As seniors, the amount of money coming in is often somewhat fixed. Correspondingly, many available income sources will be less than the incomes we enjoyed before we became elderly. But some additional income may be better than none. In fact, the shortfall in cash flow may be small enough to be funded for a period by income sources accessible to seniors.

Here are some thoughts about earning some additional revenue:

- Teach. Tutor a struggling student. Be an instructor for ESL (English as a Second Language) programs. Teach children to play instruments including the piano. One senior woman taught neighbor children to play the guitar.
- Organizations that frequently employ seniors. Costco and Sam's Club retain the elderly to provide food samples. Likewise, Walmart employs seniors to be greeters. Ushers at a regional playhouse theatres or symphony halls are often elderly. Museums utilize older people to watch over portions of the facility or to give tours. Elementary-school crosswalk guards are an option. Mortuaries frequently pay seniors to do small tasks, be greeters, and staff evening viewings. Movie theatres often hire older people during the weekdays when their high-school employees are in school. Minor-league

baseball stadiums employ seniors to help people locate their assigned seats.
- AmeriCorps Seniors is a U.S. Government program that can help seniors find small-paying jobs as either "senior companions" or "foster grandparents." In both areas, the small monthly compensation does not impact federal or state assistance. Or visit your local Workforce Services, Easter Seals, or Goodwill Office. Each employs seniors.
- Some companies support older employees. Several women in their 70s and 80s found a small confectionary company that hired part-time people in their age group to hand-wrap candy. The work was not physically taxing. They loved the association with the other employees of all ages. The women enjoyed contributing to the business. A few extra dollars each week came in handy. Getting out of the house several days a week was a big plus. You never know if you can find such employment opportunities unless you look for them.
- SSI Program. "Supplemental Security Income" is a program administered by the Social Security Administration, which is designed for children and adults that have a permanent disability as well as some adults over 65. To qualify, the individual must have limited income or resources. If applicable, check it out through the Social Security website.
- Think outside the box. One elderly divorced woman with an acting background became connected to a large medical school. She became an actress for

hospital training videos. In addition, she was paid to be on a panel each semester. The panel's topic was, "How doctors should talk to elderly patients about sexual relations."

C. Money Going Out (Expenses)

The other approach to the money equation is to look for ways to reduce expenses. Depending upon your circumstances, an adjustment in your lifestyle may be required. Spending levels during your employed years may not be sustainable forever. Tightening your financial belt may be required.

Begin by tracking where you spend your money each month. Group the expenditures into categories, like housing, transportation, food, utilities, insurance, entertainment, clothing, gifts, charitable donations, etc. Once you can see where your money is going, areas of potential savings may become obvious.

Here are some cost-cutting thoughts:

- Housing costs are often a major portion of your cash outflow. Even if you have lived in the same house for decades, downsizing might make sense.
- Do you eat out a lot? Restaurants, including fast food chains, are much more expensive than preparing meals at home.
- Car costs can be expensive. Car payments, insurance, gas, and maintenance can add up. Do senior couples really need two cars? Less costly cars may also be available. Less mileage traveled can help.

Dispelling Worries

- Cable TV bills can be excessive.
- Do you need both a landline telephone as well as a mobile phone? Would a cheaper cell phone plan make more sense?
- Insurance costs may be a pocket of opportunity. If needed, have someone who is financially savvy review your insurance contracts.
- Are your gifts to grandchildren (or great grandchildren) beyond your budget? Be careful not to give away more than is prudent.
- Look for senior discounts at fast food or sit-down restaurants and movie theaters. Some grocery stores have double coupon days. Find government subsidies on some food items.
- Curtailing travel may be required. Taking a cruise or touring with a group may no longer be viable options. Or do so less frequently.

Financial Help

At some point your children may take over managing your checkbook. Kim's mother asked Rich to handle her finances in her last years. He could immediately see that Della Mae had been donating to every charity that sent her a request. These charities probably shared her contact information, as her mailbox was filled with requests. He also discovered that a monthly magazine had regularly sent her premature renewal notices, which she dutifully paid. At that point, her subscription had been renewed through the next two decades. Having someone take over the paying of bills might help to get spending in line with income. Removing that burden may be a welcome relief.

As much as you might hate it, your children might need to help financially. Their assistance may come in the form of offering a room in their home, paying for a portion of your senior living center monthly rent, or simply providing cash to get you out of a hole.

Debts

What if you have debts instead of savings? If that is your circumstance, the above suggestions regarding incoming and outgoing cash flow may be of some help. Interest payments, particularly if they are for credit card balances, can be a heavy load to bear. If needed, let others help you figure out a plan.

We are not advocating personal bankruptcies. But some use that legal approach to reduce their financial challenges. See an attorney, CPA, or financial advisor if you wish to understand the implications of that legal action.

2. Family

All families have challenges. Nobody's family is perfect. In-law children, with their own personalities and family circumstances, can add complexity to the situation. Family disagreements can cause trauma for you and the rest of your family members. So, what can we do about it?

Begin by recognizing that problems exist in every family. The fact that your family is not ideal does not make you an awful parent or a bad grandparent. Each adult within a

Dispelling Worries

family must make their own choices in life. The elderly family member cannot live the lives of their offspring for them. Many family problems are not fixable by elderly parents.

One son struggled with substance addictions for several decades. His aging parents, however, continued their encouragement and unconditional love. After decades and two failed marriages, this son finally was able to maintain recovery from his addiction. Long after his parents were dead, he kept a picture of the two of them in his kitchen to remind himself of their support.

The parents of a daughter in a troubled marriage recognized that she was headed for a divorce from her opioid-addicted husband. So, instead of downsizing their home, they built a larger home with a basement designed to house their daughter and her children. Their foresight proved to be a safe and welcome solution to a difficult situation.

An elderly parent worried constantly about her children's troubles. She was consequently overwhelmed with situations over which she had no control. Sleep for her was difficult. Her health was failing. She was continuously on edge. Solutions to her children's problems were beyond her reach or even her influence. She simply had to "let go" and allow them to live their own lives. Not until she realized that she could not impact the outcome of any of the troubles of her family members did she finally relax. Over time, several of the then-existing problems somewhat improved. She became noticeably calmer. New problems surfaced for her children, but she was better able to manage.

Adult children coming home

On occasion, adult children move back in with their parents when the parents are in their 70s and 80s. Illnesses of either the adult child or the parent can require a move-in. Sometimes a deployed military spouse causes the remaining stateside family members to return home. Unemployment can leave the adult child with no other good options. The death of a spouse can force the surviving spouse to seek help. Or an ugly divorce can be the cause. Sometimes, parents can fear that their child is a suicide risk when alone.

We appreciate the parents who step in to help a struggling adult child. No one hopes for or even expects that an adult son or daughter will return home. We salute those that support and assist adult children who are experiencing difficult circumstances.

Thoughts for Caregivers

Family members may need to be a little cautious about another family member that moves in for financial reasons with elderly parents. Particularly if the parents are incapacitated and/or there is only one elderly parent, financial foul play could be possible. The problem may come in the form of simple requests for money. In the extreme, the person may attempt to obtain control of financial resources or the power of attorney. Every situation is unique, and trouble is not certain to happen. Just be a bit cautious and mindful.

Dispelling Worries

Providing money

Middle-aged parents, while still earning a living, have various philosophical approaches about financially supporting their children following high school graduation. At some point, all of one's children are hopefully financially on their own. Thereafter, requests for monetary assistance may, from time to time, continue. Parents, before becoming elderly, have different methods for handling these intermittent or even on-going appeals from adult children. Since the variations of the corresponding circumstances are endless and since the parents are still earning their own living, we make no comments on how best to manage these situations. Once the parents become elderly, however, requests for financial support may need to be addressed differently. The remaining comments in this section pertain to the elderly.

Once a person becomes elderly, providing temporary assistance to adult children may still make sense, but only if resources permit. Care must be taken not to deplete retirement funds, which are difficult for the elderly to replace. Frustratingly, capable adult children can sometimes desire that their elderly parents financially support them over an extended period of unemployment. A son or daughter's unreasonable expectations in their job search about compensation and level of duties often contribute to the duration of the requests. A lack of effort or misguided direction can also come into play. Unfortunately, some of these situations can place financial distress upon elderly parents.

Tough love is so hard to apply. Giving even a small amount of money can generate an avalanche of financial requests. Co-signing on car loans or even mortgages may be sought. Some children want to access a future inheritance early, thereby depleting retirement savings or setting up frustration with other siblings. One father's willingness to financially help one married daughter ballooned into helping all of his children. One 87-year-old mother, had to find a job to support her unemployed and unmotivated divorced son. One simple solution for the elderly is to say, "No," even if the request is small. In fact, particularly if the appeal is minimal, a negative response may prevent a long-term pattern of requests.

Particularly troublesome are requests of the elderly to help finance a business. Most small enterprises fail. Most family-provided funds to support new ventures eventually evaporate. Unless you have extra money you can lose, you should avoid supporting a business investment request. If you have multiple children, you may want to access the opinions of your other children before succumbing to a business investment request from one. Odds are likely that any money provided to fund a child's business venture will not be returned.

Family disputes

Frequently, adult siblings can have various levels of frustration with each other. The causes can be diverse and long lasting. An elderly parent generally has no control over these damaged sibling relationships. Sometimes, the frustrations are directed at the elderly parents. Whatever the

Dispelling Worries

cause and whoever are involved, family squabbles are unpleasant.

Here are some thoughts:

- Care must be taken not to take sides in disputes between your children. Do not try to force positive solutions.
- Adult children are frequently not open to counsel from their parents or grandparents. So, unless asked for guidance, silence is generally the best course of action. A listening ear, conversely, can be a godsend.
- Unconditional love does wonders when nothing else works.
- Your own divorce may have added complexity to your family's relationships. Often children and grandchildren become aligned with one parent or the other. The divorced parties must work together regarding their children and grandchildren. Each situation is unique with its own set of challenges. Your efforts to be generous, forgiving, and willing to work together for the good of your posterity will hopefully pay long-term dividends.
- Divorces of your children can be messy for everyone. We have seen elderly parents continue to emotionally support the ex-son/daughter-in-law in addition to supporting their blood relatives. Maintaining in-law relationships can be very helpful in your interactions with the grandchildren. Paul and Della Mae's support of their ex-daughter-in-law came full circle. After Della Mae became widowed, she eventually went to live with her son's former wife. This caregiver was a

retired hospice nurse. She welcomed her former mother-in-law when the options of living with her own children did not work out. That positive living arrangement remained in place during the last year of Della Mae's life.

- Do not demonstrate favorites among your children or grandchildren. Damaged feelings, once embedded, are hard to erase. At times, feelings of favoritism arise even when you work hard to treat all family members without bias. If all else fails, do your best. Keep trying. Do your best.
- Be careful not to generate or perpetuate family gossip. Talk positively about family members to other family members. Keep your negative opinions to yourself. Keep confidences confidential.
- Some of your children and grandchildren may move away from your hometown or home state. Some parents feel compelled to constantly encourage these offspring to return. Having been on the receiving end of such encouragements, we recommend keeping those sentiments to yourself. Acceptance and support for those who have moved will be appreciated. "Distant" relatives do not want to feel less loved. Geographic distance requires special efforts to maintain positive relationships.

3. News Reports

News reports, whether worldwide, national, or local, generally focus on negatives. For a story to be newsworthy, it often depicts the worst that society has to offer. Wars, crimes (including mass shootings), natural disasters, and political divisiveness can all paint a terribly dark picture. As we age, we can become obsessed with fears for our families, for ourselves, and for the state of global, national, and local societies.

So, here are some thoughts about what to do:
- Be conscientious and deliberate about how much and when you watch the news.
- Do not fret about negative situations over which you have no control or influence.
- Focus on things you can do to make a difference. Use your energy to support the victims of such events: the refugees, the survivors of natural disasters, or those affected by crimes. Donate, volunteer, or just pray for those who suffer.

4. Scams

Scams often personally impact seniors. While potential property thefts or violent crimes are generally more worrisome than a reality for the elderly, scams are offenses that frequently target older people.

One man in his eighties got caught in a common Africa-sourced scam, which proposed to need his help to "protect millions of dollars from bad guys." For his assistance, they proposed that he would be given a huge payment. Over a period of months, they requested several multi-thousand-dollar payments, which he dutifully sent to them. His family members tried to convince him of the fraudulent intent of this scam, but he would not listen. He even insisted that he must make a trip to Africa to assist the people requesting his help.

The elderly can be an easy prey for these and many other types of scams. Transferring responsibilities for your finances to a younger family member can be a needed protection. Talking freely with your children about proposed financial arrangements by strangers or even acquaintances can provide a safeguard. Confusing requests may be resolved by involving others you trust. Your state government likely has a department set up to help protect aging adults from scams.

Scams are a big business throughout the world as well as in your own neighborhood. Skepticism about financial requests should be high. Hanging up on phone calls that want you to do something or that want you to listen to a pitch is perfectly acceptable. Just say, "No thanks," and end the call without further conversation. You do not need to politely explain why you are not interested. Doing so only gives the scammer more of an opening to provide perplexing arguments.

Some scams can be very sophisticated. We recently received a pop-up warning on our computer screen from "Apple Security Department" that seemed very real. Our Apple computer had supposedly been hacked, and we were instructed not to touch the computer until we had called the phone number on the screen. The warning appeared to be valid, so we made the call, which was forwarded to a second call that was supposedly our bank's fraud department. The complexity and cleverness of the scam was alarming. We were both on the phone and were unsuspecting of the scam until they asked us to withdraw money from our bank account. We were instructed not to tell the bank's tellers why we were pulling out the cash because they might be involved in the fraud. We hung up on the call and then phoned the bank's actual fraud line directly. They confirmed the fraud attempt.

We then called the real Apple Support directly and received the same confirmation. The Apple technician helped us get the warning off our computer screen as well as upload the latest Apple software that had updated security protection. In hindsight as we write about the experience, it seems so obvious that it was a scam. But in real time, the fraud was initially not apparent.

During the next several hours, we received many phone calls and texts from additional scam attempts. If a warning pops up on your computer or other electronic device and tells you to call the phone number on the screen, do not call it. If the warning supposedly comes from your bank, Internet provider, or utility company, call their published customer service phone number to verify whether the request is valid.

Scams are one area that should warrant a degree of concern for the elderly. Be careful. Be mindful. Be apprehensive. Protect yourself by involving others that you trust when suspicious situations arise. And hang up on solicitations that seem dubious.

> ### *Thoughts for Caregivers*
>
> Anybody at any age can be the target of a scam or deceptive investment opportunity. Since the elderly can be more susceptible to fraudulent pitches, your warning counsel to them might help them be better prepared when a scam attempt arises. Your encouragement to them to hang up on soliciting phone calls may keep them out of trouble.

Caregiver Scams

One disturbing reality is that some family members or external caregivers take financial advantage of the seniors they are purporting to help. Financial exploitation can happen through taking control of financial resources or by having wills and/or powers of attorney changed. Involving other trusted family members can provide protection. Or the Adult Protective Services Department of your state government may be helpful. If you are uncomfortable with someone who is supposedly helping you, get others involved. Not wanting to publicly embarrass the caregiver can lead to trouble. Simply hoping the problem will go away on its own could make matters worse.

> ### *Thoughts for Caregivers*
>
> Alerting the elderly to potential problems arising from individuals whom they know may help the elderly be more cautious when confronted with requests. Appeals for cash, loans for businesses, or changes to legal documents should be vetted with more family members than just the requesting person.

Dispelling Worries

Romance Scams

We discussed romance scams in a previous chapter. Often, the motivation for these scams is financial. If your new love interest requests money before you are married, you should be concerned. If the person was previously unknown to you or others you trust, take your time to really get to know them. As suggested before, a background search might surface potential problems. Romance scams are a big business. Be careful.

Thoughts to ponder:

What worries me? What can I do about those worries?

_____

_____

_____

_____

_____

_____

_____

Life Beyond 70

Chapter 10

Calming Storms

Rich recently went to the deli department of our grocery store to order some potato salad. The lady behind the counter looked a bit worn down, and he asked her how her day was going. "Terribly," she replied. "I just made a mistake with a customer's order and the woman chewed me out royally." The customer had been very pushy and had ordered 48 pieces of chicken. When the customer repeated the order a third time, the woman behind the counter got flustered. She mistakenly rang up the cost to be $480 instead of the correct amount, which was a small fraction of that number. When the customer saw the error, she relentlessly scolded the poor clerk as the correct amount was reentered.

The unnerved worker was still shaken about the interaction when Rich came to the counter. She even showed him on the weighing machine how she had made the mistake. Rich encouraged her to let it go. The problem would have been discovered before the customer left the store. Hence, the mistake could have had no lasting consequences. He got her to laugh about it when he studied the potato salad ticket to see if the cost was going to be $480. A simple error had unfortunately been made to sound terrible by the angry customer.

How do we respond when someone's mistake affects us? Do we react angrily? Or are we kind in the face of a troubling situation? When we are the one who made the mistake, we appreciate the graciousness of the recipient of our error.

Becoming old is not for the faint of heart. The sum of all the physical, emotional, and social challenges can create a burden not easily or comfortably borne. Simple activities such as buttoning a button or tying one's shoes may become difficult. We wake up each morning waiting to find if a new pain will afflict us. Our irritation about small things can lead to becoming incensed about almost everything. Anger can build upon itself. We can spiral down to becoming our worst selves.

Let us throw out some real-life frustrations:

- We wait a long time to see a doctor. Since we have an increasing amount of scheduled doctor visits, our cumulative wait time can become excessive.
- A waitress mixes up our order. We asked for wheat toast, and she brought us white. We requested a new napkin or a ketchup bottle, and the busy waitress forgot.

Calming Storms

- Somebody cuts us off in traffic or drives too closely behind us.
- Our family is not as responsive as we would like them to be. Their busy lives have priorities that do not match our needs.
- Our hairdresser or barber seems to have lost their touch.
- Meals prepared for us are less than stellar. Food does not match our preferences. Our taste buds remember things tasting better when we were younger.
- Certain people annoy us.
- The opposing political party is ruining our country.
- Room temperatures are either too hot or too cold.

Thoughts for Caregivers

Caregivers who support the elderly can also build up a mountain of frustration. Sacrifices made to accommodate an older person can go unappreciated. The elderly and their caregivers are not always aligned. Acceptable compromises can be difficult to achieve. The annoyance of dealing with the elderly can shorten the fuse for everyone involved. Both the caregiver as well as the elderly can become unsettled. When confronted with an irritating situation with an elderly person that you support, take a deep breath. Remind yourself of their age. Try to be gracious even when it is hard.

Life is full of trials of various sizes. Some are insignificant and trivial. Others, while consequential, are beyond our control or influence. Our senior years can be particularly difficult. Becoming angry is a choice. Choosing not to become agitated is a learned behavior that is valuable at any age.

Managing Negativity

What can we do to reduce our anger? Here are some simple techniques to get us back in control of our negative emotions:

- Take a deep breath, and then slowly exhale while smiling. If needed, repeat three times.
- Look for ways to compliment those with whom you have small interactions. A kind word can make somebody's entire day, as well as our own.
- Count your blessings. Write them down. Gratitude for positives can cause negatives to subside.
- One emergency-room doctor decided to have "Thankful Thursdays." He was a religious man, so on Thursdays, he chose to only thank God for his blessings without asking for anything in return. That effort really helped his attitude throughout the week.
- Solve the underlying problem. Sometimes we have legitimate concerns. And often, those concerns seem to diminish in importance or become less "legitimate" when we work to fix them.
- Catch yourself before becoming irritated over future anticipated conflicts. Frequently, these clashes never materialize.

We recently saw painted on the window of a small Mexican restaurant the following bit of South-of-the-border wisdom:

"Inhale tacos. Exhale negativity."

While we do like tacos, the more helpful part of this advice is to "Exhale negativity." If you must eat tacos to get that result, we recommend ordering a large portion. "Exhaling negativity" is a solution that is good for all of us.

<u>Forgiveness</u>

In the New Testament, Jesus teaches the importance of forgiving others. In fact, he takes the effort to an extreme when he commands his disciples to forgive an offending person seventy times seven. The total times we are to forgive an offense are a whopping 490 times. He was clearly commanding his followers to never stop forgiving. Why would he encourage something that is so difficult? Whether or not you are a Christian, what is the benefit of forgiving others?

One of the most debilitating activities we can internalize is anger against someone who has offended us. The perpetrator is rarely affected by our anger. Although we fume and fuss and simmer, the only person impacted by our frustration is ourselves. Most of the wrongdoings are long forgotten by the instigator and frequently not even recognized by that person at the time of their transgression. If all the infractions against us over the course of a lifetime were added up, we would have a huge pile of self-pity. How do we get rid of this obstacle? The answer is simple while the execution is difficult. That answer is forgiveness. Plain and simple, we just need to let it go. Move on. Stop thinking about it. Forgive. Fully forgive. And forget.

Some problems must be addressed. These situations can be challenging but ignoring them does not work. The story is told of two brothers who lived in a single-room cabin in the woods for decades. At one point they became angry with each other and painted a line down the middle of the cabin. For years, neither brother spoke to the other nor crossed the line into the other's territory. In the end, neither could remember what had first caused the disagreement. How sad to let pent up anger produce two miserable and lonely lives. While this example is an extreme, working out issues with somebody with whom you are angry is often the best course of action.

Surgical Mishaps

One man in his 70s experienced two cataract surgeries, one on each eye that failed miserably. The administering surgeon mishandled both surgeries so badly that the man's eyesight was thereafter irreparable. Other doctors consistently expressed their dismay at the badly performed surgeries for which they had no solution. The operations permanently eliminated the man's ability to read and do other normal functions.

The man was understandably furious. For several years, he stewed continuously over the surgeon's mistakes. Finally, the man's son encouraged him to forgive the surgeon. Taking his anger with him to his grave would not make things better. The man knew that his son was right, but considerable determination was required to corral his bitterness and change his "heart" toward the surgeon. With substantial effort the man succeeded in achieving the needed forgiveness and lived out his last decade with calmness and compassion. This story of forgiveness was shared at the man's funeral along with his other amazing character traits. Forgiveness was just one of many of the man's stellar attributes.

Over a lifetime, a person may experience several less-than-successful surgical procedures. Some are the mistakes of good hard-working physicians that are normally successful. Others are performed by over-booked surgeons who simply do not allow the needed time to do things correctly. A few are the result of incompetent doctors who probably should not be practicing. And at times, our own bodies fail to recover in a pattern that the medical industry would consider normal. Whatever the cause, patients can experience surgical results that underperform their expectations. Anger can be easy and plentiful. Forgiveness is difficult. But without forgiveness, the anger can negatively affect the quality of our remaining years. If ever forgiveness were needed, these difficult circumstances require it.

Family Disputes

Disputes within a family are not unusual. Often, the offending party is an adult sibling or an adult son or daughter. Disagreements can occur. Fissures can disrupt. Non-speaking time-periods can stretch on. Sleights can build in magnitude and momentum. While never easy, forgiveness may not make the relationship perfect, but the ache of the dispute can be dissipated.

Abusive Situations

Considerable mistakes by some parents can sometimes overwhelm the children long after the victims have become adults. Some of these problems are devastating to the wounded with life-long consequences. Even the elderly can be burdened by the mistakes of earlier generations. Without diminishing these tragic actions, the call for forgiveness remains both valid and therapeutic.

Thoughts for Caregivers

Forgiveness may also be required by a caregiver. Some elderly parents had serious shortcomings as they navigated parenthood. And now, the burden of caregiving support to that person has fallen on us. Memories of frustrations during our growing up years cascade upon us. Hence, abundant forgiveness is needed. Without forgiveness, the caregiving effort will constantly remind us of mistakes they made years ago. Even beyond that person's mortal existence, our frustrations can continue to trigger ill feelings toward them. As hard as it may be, forgiveness is both necessary and therapeutic.

Thoughts to ponder:

What frustrates me the most? What can I do about it?

_____

_____

Who do I need to forgive? How do I plan to achieve that forgiveness?

Life Beyond 70

Chapter 11

Moving On

One woman in her nineties agonized over omissions she thought she had made as a mother and grandmother. She felt she could have done better. She reiterated her shortfalls regularly to her friends and family. Finally, one of her daughters said, "When you talk like that, Mom, it makes us feel like failures and that you are disappointed in how we turned out." That message did wonders in stopping the woman from fixating on her regrets.

Every person has made mistakes. As we age, we sometimes reflect on what we could have done differently. We wish we could turn back the clock and have a do-over. Since time travel is not an option, what can we realistically do? How can we reconcile past actions so that we can move forward in life?

Several simple steps can help. Note that none of the steps call for public confessions to everyone who will listen.
1. **Acknowledge the mistake. Make a real effort to change.**
2. **Feel sorrow for it.**
3. **Do your best to make true restitution.**
4. **Do not repeat it.**
5. **Forgive yourself.**

None of these steps are easy. None can be skipped.

Unfortunately, you may not be able change other people's perceptions of your past failings. Everyone makes mistakes, some larger than others. People can change. You can change. But sometimes, others cannot let go of your past errors. We can learn from Charles Dickens' character, Ebenezer Scrooge. Most of us only remember Scrooge from the beginning of the story when he was a greedy and hard-hearted person. We tend to forget that he transformed through the experiences in the story to be a very likeable and generous man. You may have the same experience where others focus on your past mistakes. You cannot force others to recognize the changes in you. So, once you have reconciled with yourself, let it go. Do your best. Do not repeat the errors you made in the past. Do not let sadness for your prior mistakes overwhelm you now. Move on.

Thoughts to ponder:

What regrets weigh heavily on me? What can I do about them?

_____

_____

_____

_____

_____

_____

_____

_____

Chapter 12

Managing Healthcare

At one point in Rich's business career, he was responsible for the marketing activities of Snickers Bar, the candy brand. In those days, the marketing team often targeted their promotional and advertising activities towards individuals who ate abnormally large amounts of Snickers Bars. These unique Snickers lovers were referred to as "heavy-users." Amazingly, these consumers ate an average of three "king-size" Snickers Bars a day.

The term "heavy user" could easily be applied to the elderly as it pertains to the medical industry. During our lives, we all go through periods of intense dealings with healthcare services. Generally, those interactions intensify in magnitude and frequency as we age.

Many who have enjoyed good health in their pre-elderly years hope and even assume this pattern will continue as they age. Rich's mom enjoyed superb health until her 70s.

She was rarely ill and had no broken bones or surgeries throughout her life. She simply presumed her good fortune would continue indefinitely. But like most of us, her decades beyond 70 were filled with health challenges. Parkinson's disease was a shock as well as congenital heart failure. Urinary tract infections became common for her. She had no joint replacements, but broken bones from falls with corresponding surgeries became regular occurrences. In a nutshell, she experienced "normal" health conditions for elderly people.

Most elderly face unprecedented health issues, unprecedented for them while being common to this age group. Cancer, joint replacements, heart disease, serious illnesses, back troubles, and cognitive loss problems are all possibilities. Eye, ear, and skin challenges can happen. Since we are probably going to be working more closely with medical-care providers, we should seek to become proficient at doing so.

We will address the issues outlined below:

1. **Doctors**
2. **Expecting the Worst**
3. **Managing Medications**
4. **Declining Eyesight**
5. **Hearing Loss**
6. **Dermatology**
7. **Joints**
8. **Sleep**
9. **Nutrition**
10. **Falling**
11. **Medical Alert Devices**

12. Depression
13. Life-threatening Illnesses
14. Insurance

1. Doctors

As we age, physicians become an ever-increasing component of our lives. Obviously, some doctors are better than others with elderly people. Aging organs grow tired and less functional. Medical difficulties can be independently serious or come like stormy waves. With simultaneous challenges, prescription medicines to resolve one problem can interfere with those intended to address another. We applaud those physicians who are adept at working with seniors.

After bouts with three types of cancer, Rich's dad had had enough. Dolan was now in his nineties, sitting yet again in another doctor's office in a cancer center. The physicians were amazing. A caring, interested, engaged team of doctors was once again convened with Dolan and his two children to see what options would be best. But Dolan was done. He had been through too many treatments that succeeded in preserving his life while simultaneously reducing the quality thereof. So, after listening to what the physicians had to say, he simply announced that he would no longer be having treatments. The doctors persisted. They could do more. Dolan, however, was finished. Finally, during a pause as the physicians contemplated what would be best to do next, Dolan summed up the situation. "That's a wrap," he announced. He then stood and walked out the door. His treatments were complete.

After a few months of struggling, Dolan was gone. He was ready to be done. More delaying-treatments were not his selected option. If the quality of his life could not be restored, then he did not want his life to be preserved. The elderly should have a choice in their medical treatments.

Despite Dolan's decision to forgo further cancer treatments, we greatly appreciated the team of dedicated doctors who were so conscientious about working with a patient in his nineties. Not every doctor has that luxury. Doctors working for large medical corporations can be under serious pressure to move quickly through each patient's evaluation. Our daughter-in-law is an ophthalmologist in New York City. Recently, she quit her job with a large medical provider because the pressure to quickly evaluate each patient was inhibiting her ability to provide care. She was loaded with so many patients that she had insufficient time to even dilate each patient's eyes properly before diagnosing what was wrong.

Similarly, we had a primary-care physician who was fired from his employment with a large medical company because he took too long with each patient. We followed him to his next employer because his help was so valuable. In contrast, we had an orthopedic surgeon who failed to see (or at least acknowledge) several critical mistakes when quickly reviewing a CT scan of his recent surgery on Kim's foot. These errors, however, were clear to other surgeons who were asked for their opinions. If your doctor makes their evaluations too quickly, you may have the wrong doctor. If your doctor seems to be impatient with your age, finding another doctor might be wise.

Doctor Visits

Here are some thoughts for the elderly about doctor visits:

- Write down your questions for the physician before the appointment begins.
- Have two sets of ears at doctor's appointments. Even though we listen intently, the diagnosis, as well as the directions given, is often lost before we leave the doctor's office. Have your caregiver, spouse, or friend take notes on what the doctor says. Review those notes before a follow-up visit.
- Be attentive and kind to the medical staff. Be firm with desires and concerns but not demanding.

Second Opinions

If a diagnosis or treatment does not sound right or does not seem to address the medical issues correctly, get another opinion. If the situation is complicated, get several more opinions. Do not be concerned about offending the first physician.

In attempting to resolve issues from Kim's unsuccessful foot surgery, five different surgeons proposed five completely different medical procedures. Thankfully, we did not stop seeking opinions before seeing the fifth doctor whose evaluation and proposed solution made the most sense. Other than the original surgeon who spent only ten minutes evaluating and proposing a surgical repair, all the other doctors took significant time, as much as an entire hour, thinking through, explaining the situation, and generating proposed next steps.

Wellness Exams

Before becoming elderly, we often delayed scheduling wellness exams until a problem arose. Waiting for health difficulties to surface may not be the best approach as we age. Even though we may not have had problems during our pre-elderly years, our body parts are getting older. Screening exams can reveal problems that can be resolved in their treatable stages. Get checked before you know you have a problem.

One healthy woman entering her elderly years waited over a decade to have a wellness exam. She felt fine. Why schedule a doctor visit? The results of the exam were a bit of a shock. While the primary care physician found nothing immediately life threatening, she was pre-diabetic and had high cholesterol. Her doctor was somewhat upset at her for waiting so long. The results of her exam could have been far worse.

Preventive Medicine

Some physicians seem to conclude that preventive medicine or certain screenings are no longer needed once we reach a certain age. For instance, prescribing colonoscopies or mammograms for the elderly may be deemed unnecessary. At some point those procedures may no longer be needed, but let's not accept that conclusion too early. If a doctor indicates such efforts are no longer necessary, a second opinion may be worth seeking.

2. Expecting the Worst

Fixating on potential health problems that could possibly happen can sometimes blur what challenges are really there. Rich's father, in his 80s, needed medical care and entered a busy Brooklyn hospital when visiting New York for a wedding. Unfortunately, a doctor walked into his room when Dolan was alone and read him the wrong patient's terminal diagnosis. A few minutes later when another family member was present, the embarrassed doctor apologetically returned with the correct non-fatal diagnosis. For weeks after that experience, Dolan hung onto the first message expecting a horrible outcome to suddenly appear. Fortunately, the other family member eventually persuaded him that he missed the apologetic correction.

As we age, care must be taken not to artificially add to our health challenges by anticipating what else could go wrong. Consult with your doctor to eliminate imagined problems that do not really exist. The goal is to focus on true health issues, not on anticipated potential illnesses.

One way that worries about possible future ailments are demonstrated is a propensity to go unnecessarily to the emergency room. Both Rich's dad and Kim's mother made frequent trips to the emergency room in their later years. If they did not feel well, they often insisted on going to the ER. Nine times out of ten, they were sent home after a long and tedious array of tests. For both, ER visits appeared to be comforting. Of course, for the supporting family members, these trips were worrisome and inconvenient.

Our emergency room advice is straightforward but not always easily accepted:
- Consult with your primary care doctor about non-emergencies.
- Go to an urgent care center (if one is available) for mild ailments.
- Go to the emergency room if there is truly an emergency.

3. Managing Medications

Thank heavens, we now have zillions of medicines to resolve or improve almost every ailment. Let us make some suggestions for managing medicines:
- Use a pill container with the correct pills to take each morning, noon, and night. Or use a chart to check off medications that have already been taken. Set alarms on your phone to know when it is time to take a medication. If needed, have someone organize or even administer the medicines to take.
- Set up refill orders online to avoid running out of recurring medicines.
- Write down all your medications in a place that is easily accessible to you, your family, or your caregivers. Or take photos of each drug on a cell phone and send them to your family members so that they have the information in case of an emergency.

- Be certain each of your doctors knows all the medicines you are taking to avoid dangerous complications.
- Take medicines following the prescribed timetable.

4. Declining Eyesight

Many elderly suffer from vision problems. Aging eyes tend to lose their performance capabilities over time. The elderly can lose their ability to enjoy simple pleasures including the capability to read. Watching TV or a movie can become less enjoyable. The inability to recognize faces is highly frustrating. Even seeing what you are about to eat is sometimes challenging. Driving may become unsafe. Declining vision is a frequent cause of the loss of independence.

Some vision deficiencies can be resolved or corrected. But other significant eye ailments can be longtime challenges.

Here are some thoughts:

- Set up regular eye exams, even if your vision appears to be good. Things change over time, and some problems are correctable if caught early.
- Have someone increase the font size on your cell phone. Even a landline phone can be acquired that has larger numbers.
- Use audio or large-print books, which are available through public libraries.

5. Hearing Loss

Hearing loss creates a difficulty to connect socially. The person can feel detached and alone even while sitting in a large group. So much of life is missed when we cannot follow conversations going on around us.

Rich's dad had noticeable hearing loss in his early forties. Dolan, unfortunately, waited close to 25 years before getting his first hearing aids. Why did he wait? Vanity probably had something to do with it. But for years, he missed many of the conversations held around him. Once he finally got hearing aids, he was amazed at how the quality of his life improved. Dolan then acquired a lapel speaker that Shirley could wear to amplify her soft voice directly into his hearing aids.

Here are some suggestions:
- Have regular hearing tests. A base line of hearing results is useful to determine the rate of decline.
- Once you decide to get hearing aids, shop around. Hearing aids come in various qualities with many features and at corresponding prices.
- Closed caption TV and movies are a huge help.
- Many outside venues make accommodations for the hearing impaired. Movie cinemas and regional theatres sometimes allow patrons to listen directly through the T-coil in their hearing aids.
- Telephones exist that visually transcribe onto a screen the discussion being held on the phone. This feature allows the hearing-impaired to concurrently read the phone conversation they are having. Once

the phone call is completed, a transcript of the call can be reviewed to catch the details that may have been missed.
- Cell phones can be set up to go directly to your hearing aids.

6. Dermatology

Today's elderly grew up when concerns about excessive exposure to the sun did not exist. The more sun the better. Skin protection was never used. Consequently, skin cancer is an issue for this generation of elderly. We have two senior friends who spent considerable time in the sun in their early years. One has had over 70 surgeries on his face, and the other has had over 30. Neither schedule screening appointments with their dermatologist now. Instead, both simply regularly schedule surgical time for their next set of skin surgeries.

Skin screenings are simple and fast. If you have not visited a dermatologist before, we suggest a screening might be wise. Sorry to be blunt, but skin cancer, depending upon the kind, can be lethal.

7. Joints

Joints can wear out as we age. Replacements are common. Rotator cuff surgery is frequent as well. Finding the right surgeon is important. Sports medicine orthopedics are often good at these surgeries. Get some recommendations before you choose a surgeon. A second opinion would be smart.

Kim, who was healthy and 70, had trouble recovering from the foot surgery referenced earlier. Her painful foot was affecting her gait, which impacted her hip. The surgeon's assistant, without any evaluation of her hip, quickly suggested that she was "old enough" to probably need a hip replacement. Kim firmly informed her that was not necessary, and the assistant backed off from her hasty, age-related conclusion. Subsequent physical therapy on her foot resolved the pain in her hip. The patient's age is never a sufficient diagnosis that joints need to be replaced.

8. Sleep

The inability to get a full night's sleep can be problematic. The issue is particularly challenging for the elderly. Getting up to take a bathroom break is an increasing occurrence as we age. Arising because we cannot sleep is also a common problem. The amount of sleep required as we age can vary up or down. Many suffer from sleep apnea. If you cannot figure out a solution to your lack of sleep, medical help should be accessed.

Here are some suggestions regarding sleep:
- Finding a way to decompress at the end of each day is generally helpful. Try counting your blessings, relaxing every muscle, listening to comforting music, or reading a soothing book. Taking a warm shower or bath can also be relaxing.

    Rich's parents, in their later years, found a routine that was helpful for them. They ended each day by watching an old rerun of the TV series "M.A.S.H."

After some laughs, they were relaxed and ready for bed. Kim's dad achieved the same result by watching the Discovery Channel. Kim's mother, on the other hand, watched a political news channel every night before retiring. Consequently, Della Mae frequently experienced a poor night's sleep. Was watching the political news the cause? She was rarely relaxed before retiring to bed at night. If the last event of the evening raises your blood pressure, you are generally not going to sleep very well.

- Set a schedule when you will retire. Prepare your room for a restful sleep. Make sure it is dark enough and has the correct sleeping temperature. Figure out how to manage external noises possibly with "white noise" to drown out other sounds.
- Save your bed for sleeping. Do not read, watch TV, or take phone calls in bed. When you are in bed, it is time to sleep. When it is not time to sleep, get out of bed.

9. Nutrition

All would agree that a person's nutrition impacts their health. Unfortunately, opinions diverge greatly about the details of what we should consume. Through the years, dietary advice about what constitutes healthy foods has varied greatly. For centuries, smoking was considered a healthy activity. When we were children, some nutritionists temporarily concluded that eggs were bad for us. Rich was running a large nut company at one point in his career.

About that time, a popular view briefly surfaced that nuts were unhealthy to eat. One current debate is focused on the benefits of dairy vs. non-dairy products.

Dietary opinions, as well as fad diets, come and go. Eating a balanced diet in moderation (including fruits and vegetables) appears to be enduring advice. Add to that counsel an avoidance of too many prepackaged frozen dinners and/or fast-food meals.

As we age, our taste buds can change. Some foods just do not taste as good as when we were younger. Rich's father had problems with the meals during several weeks that he was in a rehab facility. Dolan was recovering from an ailment that reduced the kinds of foods that tasted good to him. The solution was Wendy's chili. He loved the chili sold by that fast-food chain. His family brought him chili with almost every visit. Dolan lived mostly on chili for several weeks before he could return to his senior living center. A diet exclusively of Wendy's chili is less than ideal, but it worked temporarily for him.

Much has been written about the importance of staying hydrated as a senior. Since bathroom breaks become increasingly frequent, some seniors limit their water intake. Prescribed "water" pills can add to the challenge. The proper amount of daily water to be consumed should be discussed with your doctor.

10. Falling

As mentioned earlier in the book, not wanting to look old, Rich's mother repeatedly refused to use a walker.

Managing Healthcare

Unfortunately, over a six-year period, Shirley fell four times and broke at least one bone each time. Although vanity was her standard excuse, most of her falls were in her apartment, away from public view. Dolan was still with her. But repeatedly, she found herself on the ground waiting for the ambulance to pick her up. After the fourth injury event, she finally acquiesced to using a walker. The result was that she stopped falling. That positive outcome lasted for a long period until she was in her early nineties. Her last fall came because she refused to use her walker when selecting clothes to wear. She fell backwards in her closet because she had nothing with which to steady herself. As a result of hitting her head on the floor, her health soon declined until she passed away.

In contrast, Dolan, observing his wife's falling mishaps, started using a walker before he ever tumbled. Until the day he passed away, he never fell.

Even in senior living centers, the most frequent cause of health problems is falling. Many residents have an affliction that caused them to move into the center. Yet, once they become residents, falling is the greatest challenge to remaining healthy. Most falls occur in their apartments when moving only a short distance. Unfortunately, many wait until their first fall before succumbing to using a walker. The recurring question is to what extent non-walker users will be injured in that first fall. Using a walker before the first fall can save serious injuries.

In addition to walkers, we also have several other suggestions for a person's home or apartment to reduce the risk of falling:

- Remove all throw rags. Clear and enlarge walkways by removing excessive furniture.
- Eliminate electrical cords that cross walkways.
- If you use an oxygen machine, place your oxygen tubing so that it is not a trip-hazard.
- Keep your telephone close to you so you do not have to get up to answer the phone.
- Add grab bars for stability to your bathroom and shower to assist in those danger areas.

<u>Stairwells</u>

Stairwells can be a serious hazard. Falling on stairs is a common occurrence for the aged. The ideal senior person's residence has no stairs within the living spaces. If stairs are part of the home, handrails on both sides reduce the risk. Most people fall in stairwells while carrying something. If possible, avoid transporting things that affect your balance, preclude the use of handrails, and reduce visibility of where you are placing your feet. Or better yet, move to a residence that has no stairwells.

<u>11. Medical Alert Devices</u>

Elderly people living alone need a medical alert button around their neck or on their wrist. Stories abound of people falling and laying helplessly for hours because they could not reach their phone. We are amazed at how many elderly who live alone do not have this simple precautionary device. Even those who live in senior living centers need these alert buttons.

Managing Healthcare

> ### *Thoughts for Caregivers*
> Frequently, the caregiver is the one who insists on getting a medical-alert button for the elderly that live alone. What better birthday or holiday gift could a caregiver provide to an aging loved one than a medical-alert button?

An inexpensive alternative to a medical-alert button is a phone app that detects when the person falls (or when the phone is dropped). That sudden movement triggers an alert to a loved one who can then call back to make sure the elderly person is okay. Of course, this devise only works when the person is carrying the phone. Since most elderly people do not constantly carry their cell phone, the app has limitations. A smart watch with the same app would probably be a better option.

Senior living centers generally offer alert buttons to their residents. Unfortunately, the buttons are regularly used for non-emergencies. Anytime a resident wants any kind of assistance, whether trivial or critical, the button is pushed. Eventually, the CNAs respond to the button, but at night, the staff headcount is reduced. Since the responders cannot tell an emergency from a simple request, they never know where to place their priorities. Having a separate device, which is dedicated to emergencies, would be helpful.

One woman fell in her senior living center room late at night and gashed open her forehead. Seriously bleeding, she repeatedly pressed her center-provided alert button. The limited nighttime staff was busy helping others. Her emergency was not recognized. Fortunately, she was also wearing an Apple Watch, and her daughters were thereby alerted that she had fallen. They phoned the front desk of the center and insisted that their mother needed immediate assistance. The Apple Watch probably saved her life.

12. Depression

Depression is common as we age. It is not a state of unhappiness or sadness but is a true disease. Depression is caused by a decrease in chemicals that transmit signals in the brain and is referred to as a mood disorder. Many viable treatments exist including prescription medicines and psychiatry or psychology therapies. In her 80s, Kim's mom struggled with bouts of depression that were successfully treated with anti-anxiety prescriptions.

Go see your primary care physician if you suspect this could be an issue.

Thoughts for Caregivers

Frequently, depression is easier to recognize in others and more difficult to self-diagnose. The potential symptoms are many and diverse including:
* Feeling depressed or withdrawn or irritable.
* Feelings of hopelessness or pessimism.
* Feelings of guilt, worthlessness, or sadness.
* Speech changes or slow thinking.
* Change in eating, sleeping, or daily hygiene habits.
* Angry outbursts or frustration over small matters.
* Changes in a person's normal behavior.
* Thoughts of death or suicide.

13. Life-Threatening Illnesses

Unfortunately, the longer a person lives, the more likely they will contract at least one life-threatening disease. That said, many often continue to live meaningful and worthwhile lives after they develop a catastrophic illness. With modern treatments, many can recover or at least extend their constructive lives for many months or even years.

The obvious first step is to access the best medical treatments available. Beyond healthcare solutions, here are some suggestions for dealing with serious illnesses:

- Everyone's health situation is unique. Each person's ability to cope with severe ailments and corresponding treatments is different. The will to continue to contribute to the lives of those around you is critical.
- Accept the realities of a negative diagnosis. Work to make the best of a tough medical situation.
- Help others deal positively with your health challenges. Look for ways to serve others. Send cards. Make phone calls. Build up those around you. Others watching your example can be inspired by your valiant efforts.
- Do the things you enjoy while you can.

14. Insurance

Medical Insurance

Medicare is the primary source of health care coverage for

most Americans over the age of 65. Some retirees have private insurance from their former employer. Others purchase medical insurance through the Affordable Care Act plans. Seek advice from an insurance agency to understand the options for supplemental medical insurance as well as prescription, dental, and vision policies. For those who live in other lands, socialized medicine or other government programs may solve your medical insurance needs.

Long-term Care Insurance

We are not fans of long-term care insurance. Our bias comes from Rich's parents paying into such a plan for decades. Once we thought they should be able to access the coverage, they received the run-around for years before they could "qualify" to receive any payments. Maybe they had the wrong insurance provider. Maybe you might have a better experience. Do your homework.

Medicaid

Medicaid pays for medical care for Americans with very low incomes. Long-term care for people who have used most of their money for care-related expenses is also possible. See the Medicare website.

Veterans Benefits

Anyone who served in the United States Armed Forces may qualify for government benefits including health care and long-term care. Check with the Veterans Benefits Administration at www.va.gov or your local veterans office.

Thoughts to ponder:

What am I doing well to manage my healthcare needs?

_____

_____

_____

_____

_____

_____

_____

_____

What could I do differently in managing my healthcare needs?

_____

_____

_____

Life Beyond 70

Chapter 13

Now, What Was His Name?

Almost everyone suffers some form of memory loss as they grow older. In the milder forms, "senior moments" are characterized by difficulty in finding words or remembering a person's name. At the other end of the scale, Alzheimer's or dementia can attack. A myriad of variations exists from one end of the range to the other. At the difficult end of the continuum, life can be heartbreaking and challenging. Within the middle of the spectrum, we can often get along with assistance from caregivers and/or within a senior living center. We look forward to the day when medical science finds a cure for the most difficult versions of memory loss. That day cannot come soon enough.

Kim had a dear uncle who died of dementia. As the disease progressed, he remained living with his wife whom he was fortunately able to still recognize. His children and grandchildren, however, sadly became strangers to him. His ability to navigate around the town where they had lived for decades also disappeared. Amazingly, for several months, he was able to retain one location he could still remember. For one winter, he frequently woke up, got in his car alone, and drove 40 minutes up into the mountains to a nearby ski resort. After spending the day on the slopes, he was able to find his car and drive directly to his home. That ability did not last until the next ski season, but for that one remarkable winter, he remembered enough to ski by himself. While driving with this degree of dementia is certainly not recommended, his story demonstrates how unique each person's experience with memory loss can be.

Love Your Brain

Some suggest that the less onerous versions of memory loss can be slowed by activities to strengthen your mental capacities.

Here are some suggestions:
- Read for pleasure as well as for knowledge. Do puzzles or brainteasers. Play board games.
- Study a language. Or just learn something new every day.
- Exercise. Stop smoking. Get enough sleep. Go outside and ponder the wonders of nature.
- Learn the basics about technology. Have your grandkids teach you one new feature about your cell phone each time you see them.
- Memorize poems or scripture passages. One friend in his late eighties was exceptional at memorizing lengthy passages. A dual citizen in both the U.S. and

Now, What Was His Name?

Mexico, the man was fluent and without accent in two languages. On one occasion, he was unexpectedly asked in a church meeting to stand and recite a lengthy passage from memory. Others in the room were glad the public invitation had not been extended to them. Many feared the elderly man would be embarrassed by the request. He slowly stood and fiddled briefly with his belt buckle. Finally, after an awkward silence, he straightened and asked the requestor, "Do you want it in English or in Spanish?"

- Some researchers say that the hearing-impaired who choose to forgo hearing aids are more prone to have memory issues. If so, we have yet an additional reason to address hearing loss.
- Senior moments are sometimes simply a matter of focus. Concentrating on one thing at a time can sometimes make a difference.

Medical help is obviously needed for the extreme versions of these cognitive diseases. The progression of various forms of memory loss can be gradual. Medications do exist that can sometimes help to slow the decline of memory loss. Ask your doctor for suggestions. The Alzheimer's Association website at www.alz.org can be helpful.

Thoughts for Caregivers

Caregivers also need direction and support as they assist those with severe memory loss. Depending upon the situation, a caregiver may be needed to provide support 24/7. Burning out from the stress of caregiving is a valid concern. The Alzheimer's Association sponsors local caregiver support groups. The Association also provides frequent webinars that can be helpful. Around-the-clock information and assistance are available on their helpline. Suggested responses to dementia-related behaviors are available as well as tips for successfully communicating during all stages of Alzheimer's disease. Caregivers are generally inexperienced in assisting those with severe memory loss. The Alzheimer's Association can help. And it is free.

One additional important recommendation for those that are in the early stages of these diseases has to do with preparing for what is coming. While the patient is somewhat capable, many decisions need to be made about the future. None of these decisions go well if we wait until the person is mentally incapacitated. You might want to consider:

* Locating all critical documents and information, including passwords.
* Determining patient care needs now and for the future.
* Resolving financial planning needs.
* Reviewing legal considerations with an attorney.
* Making end-of-life decisions.

Go to the Alzheimer's Association website for a good list of detailed suggestions for handling each of these critical areas.

Now, What Was His Name?

Thoughts to ponder:

What do I want to do to keep my brain active?

_____

_____

_____

_____

_____

_____

_____

Chapter 14

Writing Your Final Chapter

Repeatedly, we are reminded that life is fragile. In the 1700s, Americans found death around every corner. Childbirth, childhood diseases, tuberculosis, smallpox, pneumonia, appendicitis, and polio all contributed to "premature" deaths. Only in those days, such deaths were not premature.

Now, many of the most deadly diseases from that century have been cured. We die of other causes, but usually somewhat later in life. While great progress has been achieved as evidenced by our extended life expectancy, medicine cannot solve everything. Eventually, we all get a turn at dying.

When Rich's 91-year-old father passed away, Shirley announced she was going to die as well -- in 13 days. Shirley was on hospice at the time, and she was ready to move on to the "next rodeo." To her surprise, instead of passing,

Shirley became healthier once she stopped worrying about Dolan. She came off hospice and lived for over two years before her body finally wore out. Even though life is fragile, we generally do not have a lot of say about when we die.

People can get very philosophical about death as they age, particularly once they get beyond 85. That propensity is particularly true if one's beloved spouse is gone. Many of that age did not expect to live that long. Most would prefer not to get to 100.

One widow in her nineties was so ill with the flu that she thought she would die. She was surprised when the flu subsided, and she felt better. Her cheerful comment was, "Oh, well. Better luck next time."

With each passing year, more and more of our elderly friends leave this world. Obviously, as we ourselves age, we become less and less shocked as deaths of people we care about become more common. Kim's parents died in their 80s, and they had many peers attend their funerals. In contrast, Rich's parents died in their 90s. People came to their funerals, but their peers were mostly gone.

At a senior living center where we volunteered, deaths were common occurrences. Generally, somebody passed away about every other week. Funerals for them were wonderful overviews of their earlier lives. We should have held their memorial services when they first arrived at the center so that we could have better understood and appreciated them.

As our elderly years pass by, one inevitably thinks about death and what lies beyond. If you do not believe in an afterlife, death of loved ones can be much harder to bear. If it helps to lean on our faith, please do so. Death comes to each of us, no matter our beliefs or expectations. At that point, our questions regarding an afterlife will be answered. In the meantime, let us focus on our time remaining in this life. Since death is inevitable, what can we do to prepare?

<u>You can't take it with you.</u>

We know one man who lived a raucous life. In his sixties, he bought an existing candy business for which he paid nothing! He wrote a check for $20,000 to purchase the venture, and then had his new company write him a check for the same amount. Fifteen years later, he sold the business for $206 million. Not a bad return on his zero investment. Half of the proceeds he received in stock of the acquiring company, which eventually became worthless. The other half he got in cash. He then chose to spend every penny of his fortune as quickly as he could. Somehow, he timed his death to coincide with the complete elimination of his significant wealth. You can't take it with you if you have nothing left to take.

But that begs the question: How much can you take with you? What percentage of your net worth do you get to keep? How about financial assets like stocks, bonds, or savings accounts? Can you take a business with you? What about real estate such as homes, cabins, land, and buildings? How many RVs, boats, and cars do you get to bring along? How much jewelry? With certainty, when you go, you get to take nothing with you. So, why do we work so hard to grow the value of our belongings if we do not get to keep them?

Life Beyond 70

Rich's mother grew up in the Great Depression. Shirley lived on a farm, so they did have food to eat. As the youngest child, much of her teenage years were spent alone with her parents. The one thing that really made a difference in her life in her small town was the public library that had been funded by Andrew Carnegie. Shirley often said that Carnegie was the first person she would like to meet when she died. Like all of us, Carnegie took nothing with him, but he did leave a legacy that transcended his lifetime. Carnegie built over 2500 libraries with a third located in foreign countries. In adulthood, Shirley became a beloved librarian in an elementary school. We say "beloved" because we repeatedly met people who attended that school who spoke fondly of the difference she made in their elementary school years. They should also thank Andrew Carnegie, the difference maker for Shirley.

So, where does that leave us? We all agree that you cannot take "it" with you. But you can leave "it" where it can make a difference, even if it is a small difference. Every person must make up their own mind about their belongings. But one thing no one can do is take anything with them. So, choose wisely.

Many would argue that leaving your assets to your family is the goal. That approach is by far the most common resolution to where your belongings will end up. We are certainly not advocating against leaving your possessions to your posterity. Since you cannot take anything with you, your family can be blessed by your industry. That said, the absence of infighting among family members over your possessions might be a worthy objective. Be fair. Be thoughtful. Be specific with treasures in your will. Try to think through how things will play out.

One woman had a grand piano that she wanted kept in the family. She had many grand and great-grandchildren who took piano lessons, and several played very well. But she, at one point, mentioned only one of her grandchildren to whom to give the piano. Why did she do that? Did she really love that grandchild more and the other grandchildren less? The negative implications of such a selection can be long lasting. It is best not to select a "favorite" child or grandchild when you really love all of them equally. Said differently, do you love the piano more than each of your grandchildren? If not, be careful about making the piano (or other possessions) a stumbling block for your offspring.

One elderly couple stipulated in their will that a family member must remain living in their family home. The house was old and dated and not unique. It needed significant investment to bring it up to modern standards. Once the couple was gone, their children had a dilemma to resolve. Should they agree to their deceased parents' wishes? The house, although full of family memories, was not the most logical place for the next generation to live. And what about the generation to follow? Would they in turn be "required" to live in the old house? You cannot take possessions, including houses, with you. But be careful not to saddle future generations with things that may not be important to them.

Legal Preparations

Recently, Aretha Franklin's handwritten will was discovered under the cushions on her sofa. That may not be the best location to store one's will, but at least she had one.

The legal documents you probably need are likely to include:

- Trusts for each spouse. General instructions on trust funding and administration. A trust-funding plan. Wills for each spouse. Durable powers of attorney.
- Advance healthcare directives (living wills) including HIPAA authorizations and a medical power of attorney. Resuscitation wishes should be discussed and documented.
- A guide to procedures following death.
- A list of accounts and assets, plus all the passwords.

If you are unfamiliar with some the above documents, they will be explained as you seek to prepare them. Death gets complicated for those left behind when the legal documents are not in order. Preparing the documents also allows you to decide exactly what you want to do. Several methods can be used to prepare the needed papers. The Internet can help you to learn the fundamentals. Or you can go to LegalZoom to inexpensively get the basics done. You can also hire a good tax lawyer to help you prepare the documents. To avoid frustrating your loved ones, make sure the end-of-life paperwork is complete before you die. And do not store the documents under the sofa cushions.

> ***Thoughts for Caregivers***
> You might need to encourage the preparation of the necessary legal documents. Do so before the person becomes incapacitated. Make sure you know where the documents can be found.

Hospice

Hospice is the best thing that can happen to a dying person and their loved ones. The sole objective of hospice is to make the patient as comfortable as possible until they pass away. Hospice does not treat illnesses. It makes no effort to resolve whatever is causing a person's death. Hospice neither hastens nor postpones someone's death. Paid by Medicare, hospice care costs the individual nothing. The patient, however, must be a participant in Medicare and must qualify to obtain hospice services. Various local companies that provide hospice services provide the actual service. The level of care is based on the needs of the person. Services provided include regular home help, pain and comfort medicines, death-process counseling, hospital beds, and death certification. Assistance to the caregivers is also part of the hospice benefits.

Hospice care is not even permanent if the patient improves. Rich's mom was on and off hospice several times before she finally passed on. Kim's father, on the other hand, was continuously on hospice for four years before passing. Paul qualified for the service. But his mind was strong, and he enjoyed good conversations and relationships during that period.

One requirement of hospice care is that the patient accepting these services must go off their regular medical insurance. Hospice care is for the end of life after efforts to resolve underlying illnesses have proven unsuccessful.

> ### *Thoughts for Caregivers*
> We suggest doing homework about hospice before you need the service. You will be pleased with what you learn. The Medicare website has the answers. Hospice managers are also available to meet with you to answer your questions. For hospice information go to Medicare.gov.
>
> A variation on hospice is palliative services, which can sometimes bridge the gap before one qualifies for hospice. Palliative care, like hospice, is paid fully by Medicare. Learn about available palliative assistance before it is needed. The Medicare website can help you learn more.

Funerals

Some people leave quite specific details about what they want included in their funeral services. Why not?! If you want your funeral to celebrate your life, tell your family how you want them to commemorate it.

A few instructions you might include are:

- Decide on whether you want a burial or cremation. Picking out and possibly paying for your preferred casket or urn removes that determination from your family.
- Select the mortuary you prefer and possibly pay for your burial or cremation in advance.

- Decide who you want to speak and what music you want to be sung or performed. Dictating a limit on the length of the entire funeral service might be a welcome constraint for those attending the service.
- If you served in the military, consider having the local military unit attend the internment service to have taps played and to present a U.S. flag to the surviving family members.

Conversely, one 94-year-old was highly stressed about what instructions to give her children about observing her passing. She felt responsible to determine the details of the memorial service as well as write her own obituary. That is what her deceased husband had done, but the process for her was very stressful. Fortunately, someone pointed out that her funeral services were not for her benefit since she would likely not be there. She could let the surviving family members decide how they wanted to honor her and mourn her loss. Once she understood that she did not need to plan everything, the stress was eliminated.

Local traditions and religious customs have a heavy influence on the common practices regarding honoring the dead. But nothing precludes you from being creative.

- One woman had her body cremated and instructed that her ashes be sprinkled in the Pacific Ocean. Her family rented a large boat and had an enjoyable day sharing memories of her as they leisurely floated off the California coast.
- A couple donated their bodies to medical science and took the normal mortuary expenses and

instructed their children to rent a condo at a ski resort for a family reunion.
- An owner of a large pecan orchard had his funeral held on the bluff overlooking his trees. At an appropriate point in the service, a small airplane flew by sprinkling his ashes over the orchard.
- Some are now choosing to have some of their cremated ashes made into a ring or pendant that a loved one can continue to wear.
- One widow plans to have her husband's baseball glove buried with her in her coffin. She, thereby, hopes to return it to him when she next sees him. (We are not sure it works that way, but it is worth a try.)

It is your funeral. If you have preferences, tell your family how you want them to honor you. But if the planning process stresses you, stop doing it. Let your loved ones left behind decide what they want to do.

Thoughts to ponder:

What preparations and/or decisions do I want to pursue concerning my final chapter?

_____

_____

_____

Writing Your Final Chapter

Chapter 15

Smelling The Roses

Recently, Rich hiked a "slot" canyon with a daughter and her family. Kim was recovering from her foot surgery and chose to remain in the parking lot at the trailhead. The canyon was amazing with the narrowest part being about eight feet wide with 150-foot towering cliffs above. The hike was about two miles long with a good portion of the trail running literally in the middle of a shallow stream that descended the gorge. At the narrowest part of the ravine, the creek covered the entire canyon floor and was about six inches deep. The trail was up and down, but not dangerous. Rich had his hiking poles and wore waterproof hiking sandals. He moved at his normal pace up the canyon except when hiking up the rocky streambed. The grandkids, ages 9 through 17, were mountain goats whose hiking pace on uneven terrain was much faster than Rich's. His daughter walked behind with him, and his son-in-law stopped the children every couple hundred yards to give Rich a chance to catch up.

By the time they came to the 30-step metal staircase at the first waterfall, Rich had concluded that this arrangement was not working. He proposed that he turn around and go back alone. Nobody argued against his suggestion. No one said, "Oh, Grandpa, please stay with us!" Instead, once released from waiting for their grandparent, they scampered up the staircase and quickly disappeared toward the next waterfall.

As Rich descended the canyon alone, he looked forward to getting back to Kim. After a while, he realized that he was so focused on the end of the trail, that he was ignoring the amazing beauty of the canyon. Once he caught himself, he began to enjoy the spectacular scenery of the hike.

Sometimes, the elderly approach the last chapter of their lives in the same way. They look forward to being done so that they can be reunited with loved ones gone before. The absence of age-related aches, pains, and illnesses would also be a welcome change. The trials of life can, at times, be so onerous for the aged; they fail to see the appealing scenery still around them. We need to remind ourselves to enjoy the journey even when the terrain of life is difficult.

Conclusion

Most of us get a turn at being old. In fact, many of us remain elderly for multiple decades. The senior years can be quite challenging with many new problems we had not experienced earlier in our lives. But we can still thrive, enjoy, and make a difference. Life beyond 70 can be amazing. Keep smiling. Be upbeat in the face of adversity. Become delightfully old. Breathe in. Breathe out. Enjoy every moment.

We sincerely hope the thoughts provided have been helpful. Thank you for reading. We hope you will share this book with others.

All the best,
Rich and Kim Condie

We would love to hear from you. Please email us your comments and suggestions at info@lifebeyond70.com.

If you purchased this book on Amazon, we would greatly appreciate it if you would you leave us a review. One of the best ways for us to share the book with others is to have reviews on Amazon. Thank you in advance for your support

Thoughts to ponder:

What can I do differently to enjoy the journey of my senior years?

_____

_____

_____

_____

With whom do I want to share this book?

Quotes

"Consider it done!"
    (Kelly Spilsbury, page 12)

"When you cannot do what you've always done, you do what matters most."
    (Robert D. Hales, page 13)

"By the world's measure, they (African women) have little -- except happiness. By contrast, many of us have everything -- except happiness."
    (Sherry Dew, page 13)

"I find it is better to count my blessings than to recount my problems."
    (Russell M. Nelson, page 13)

"The only way to get through life is to laugh your way through it. You either have to laugh or cry. I prefer to laugh. Crying gives me a headache."
    (Marjorie Pay Hinckley, page 13)

"Good job. Good Job."
    (Gayle M. Clegg, page 47)

"Inhale tacos. Exhale negativity."
    (La Siesta Restaurant, Peabody, MA, page 125)

"Oh, well. Better luck next time."
    (Thella Weaver, page 164)

ABOUT THE AUTHORS

As first-time authors, we are rookies at writing books, but seasoned veterans in assisting seniors. For almost three decades, we have worked closely with hundreds of people who consider themselves elderly. In three different regions of America, we have assisted and encouraged individuals who were adjusting to the aging process. Adding to our understanding, we are now both in our seventies. Hence, we write from personal as well as observed experiences. The anecdotes in this book are all true events. We hope you found them helpful in illuminating the gentle suggestions we made. As a husband-wife team, we warmly offer our encouragement to seniors and caregivers everywhere

On a personal level, we have lived all over the United States from coast to coast, top to bottom, and in-between. We have six children and sixteen grandchildren so far. We like to hike, bike, travel, spend time with our family, serve in the community, and watch live theatre and sporting events.

www.ingramcontent.com/pod-product-compliance
Lightning Source LLC
Chambersburg PA
CBHW070148100426
42743CB00013B/2848